Vision Critical Studies

General Editor: Anne Smith

THE ONSTAGE CHRIST:
Studies in the
Persistence of a Theme

THE ONSTAGE CHRIST: STUDIES IN THE PERSISTENCE OF A THEME

by

John Ditsky

VISION

Vision Press Limited
11-14 Stanhope Mews West
London SW7 5RD

ISBN 0 85478 284 2

Printed in Great Britain by
Redwood Burn Limited
Trowbridge & Esher
Typeset by Chromoset Ltd,
Shepperton, Middlesex.

MCMLXXX

Contents

Foreword

This collection of studies of significant modern plays grew out of the repeated teaching of many of them to classes of students of drama at the Universities of New York, Detroit (both in the United States), Windsor (Canada), and Oxford (at Corpus Christi College, during the University of Windsor Summer Programs of 1973, 1974, and 1978). It is based upon the observation that although this is generally supposed to be an agnostic age, the mythic pattern based upon the life of Christ has proved remarkably persistent as a means of informing a surprisingly great number of modern plays. In some cases this presence has been explored before, usually because it is obvious or authorially intended; in others, my attention will have been the first of its sort, either because the presence is more subtle or because, perhaps, it was only subconsciously intended. (It could of course be both.) Some writers (Eliot, O'Neill, Albee) are discussed because, though obvious, they could not be omitted, and because I wished to provide a consistent approach to a large body of works. My method of close readings is intended to provide the conclusions I would urge upon my readers, though I have resisted—or stopped at the point of mere suggestion—forced or contrived readings. And although I have of course read much of the relevant prior criticism, I am neither in conscious opposition nor in derivative subordination to it. In no instance do I maintain that this approach provides the major or only means of understanding the play, but in each I consider that it may prove useful in establishing the understanding that readers and theatre audiences alike are said to seek.

The general incidence of the Christ-pattern in modern drama shows great variety. It is by no means confined to the predictable figure of the sacrificial victim; there are examples that correspond to many phases of the life and career of Christ, including those of the teacher, the redeemer, the giver of love or hope or peace or justice, and of course the martyr to a cause. But the Christ-presence can also be ironical, or diffused among a number of individuals. The persistence of this usage is striking. But interesting, too, are the accompanying instances of Old Testament references—examples, most often, of rejected prophecy, which the Christ-figure must eventually confirm or justify. An underlying social, or artistic, need to be visited by a type of the Christ seems much in evidence.

But this is not a theological volume, nor one which takes any position whatever as to the validity of the pattern it discusses. It invites informed perusal—that is, a familiarity with the Biblical analogues it discusses—as well as acquaintance with the plays themselves. I hope it will reward such informed perusal. I confess an abiding fascination for the lingering, permanent, and necessary religious aspect of the theatrical experience—one which ought to remind us that the drama of the West was reborn in the re-enacting of the central statement of Christ's mission. The intimate connection between the theatre and the church in our society, I need hardly point our, is—in a way which is beyond the rightful province of this study—a clue to the nature of our deepest selves, and to their needs.

I am indebted, in the preparation of this manuscript, to the occasional and valuable advice of Father Norman G. McKendrick, S.J., as well as that of my patient wife, Sue. This book is dedicated to my parents, who are thus only indirectly responsible for any errors it may contain.

In choosing texts of plays for quotation within this volume, effort has been made to cite the best and most readily available version. While such aspects of the originals as indentation and orthography have been left unchanged, italics have frequently been omitted when their employment in the quoted editions has been arbitrary or irrelevant to their appearance in this study.

1

Ibsen's Myopic Calvary:
The Wild Duck

It is intimidating enough to be the father of anything or anybody without having to be known as "The Father of Modern Drama", yet Henrik Ibsen bears up well under the burdens of his presumed paternity. We should not expect all the distinctive themes and techniques of modern drama to be evident in the works of a single pioneer, however, especially when that pioneer was often much more interested in reshaping and reorienting the dramatic process already known as "the well-made play" than in inventing *new* forms of dramatic process. So that in opening this collection of studies with a consideration of *The Wild Duck* (1884),[1] there should be no expectation that it will prove the most important of the series that follows, the richest in its references to our chosen theme or image, nor even the best of introductions to the methods that will be pursued. *The Wild Duck* is simply the oldest play to be considered here, and Henrik Ibsen cannot fairly be excluded from consideration.

The appearance of the Christ motif in *The Wild Duck* is less than obvious. If Ibsen is heaviest-handed in employing the metaphor of sight and illusion in this play, his depiction of another motif—the sacrificial child—is somewhat more gently advanced, and yet the Christ-relationship within the play is one that may be recognized without great effort. Still, it may be argued that the theme is merely implicit, and not consciously intended. Perhaps the ideal critic of *The Wild Duck* is the drunken ex-clergyman Molvik, who recognizes in Hedwig's death a moment demanding Biblical references; and yet both of Molvik's outburts (p. 209) are silenced by the doctor, Relling, who comes as close to being Ibsen's *raisonneur* as prudent reading of the play can determine.

I intend to make such a prudent reading, one in which no wild claims for the pervasiveness of my chosen image will be put forth. Still, it is appropriate that we start with such a play, for it demonstrates how the Christ-presence that can be found in some of the best of modern theatre is seldom a conscious and deliberately included element consisting of a thirty-three-year-old Jewish male who dies on something very much like a cross so that others may live more fully. The martyr is only a part of the whole personality; many phases of the career of the historical/Biblical Jesus are of obvious significance to the overall validity of his mythical presence. That conception of the Christian type in holistic terms is thus the necessary first premise to this discussion.

The genuine Christ-figure, when one appears, is often likely to be surrounded by false or anti-Christs; and that is the case in *The Wild Duck*. On the other hand, the Christ presence is also likely to be fragmented—found among several persons—and that is also the case here. Nor are these two assertions necessarily contradictory. This play has been chosen to represent Ibsen's work even though the body of that work is full of examples of individuals who die in pursuit of an ideal; *The Master Builder* and *Brand* come immediately to mind. But *The Wild Duck* gives us something more: the presence of supposedly mature male pursuers of the Ideal who are shown to be false Messiahs by a child. This little child, then, would lead them, were they only wise enough to pay it heed. But that is unlikely, even though this particular child, Hedwig, is the character who most truly and purely accepts the "Claim of the Ideal" on individual personality. It is the play's final irony, however, that her sacrificial gesture will fail to redeem its chosen object.

That irony rests for its impact upon the linking of the Christ theme with the more obvious ones of sight and illusion in the play. For some may feel themselves called to be Christs, but few are truly chosen; and of those whose call is genuine, it may happen that their sacrificial act is prevented from having the effect it should—by defective vision. To consider fully the notion of clear-sighted pursuit of the Ideal, we would have to undertake a wide study of the Nietzschean ambience of the period in which this play was written. We *can* observe, however, that Ibsen was doing something radically different with what we will come to recognize, in modern terms, as the fundamentally "sexist" notion of the Overman. Ibsen's redemptive figures are frequently women, though Hedwig in *The Wild Duck* is barely that, but rather someone who in the act of dying establishes the fact of her adult integrity—and fixes forever, as a photograph would, its image on our consciousnesses. Hedwig can be looked upon as a gentler version of the anguished Hedda Gabler, for she too claims her life in surrendering it.

And what is sacrificed in *The Wild Duck*, as in *Ghosts*, is the figure who best represents what is usually translated as "the Joy of Life" in Ibsen's works. The sacrifice is necessitated by the inability of the persons in the play, particularly the so-called idealists, to love according to the rule of the Joy of Life. Thus, they are false idealists. What they require, and what most of us settle for, is something to take the place of a genuine Ideal, and that is (as Relling puts it) the so-called "vital lie" or "Life-Lie". (The Norwegian would seem to demand the latter, and the Eva Le Gallienne translation I am using goes so far as to call it "Basic Lie".) *The Wild Duck*, then, is a critique of the existential plight of characters who are not Brands, who are not equipped by the strength of their perception of the true Ideal for climbing, but who must manage instead, as best they can, to get along with a synthetic dream, a comforting illusion. Hedwig's death, pathetically, is on behalf of her father's need for such an *ersatz* vision of perfection.

Ibsen's use of the motifs of light and illusion in the play is almost obsessive. For instance, the opening stage-directions (p. 105) contrast the room before us, in its "subdued light" and where the dialogue of Act I will occur, with the room behind it, which is "brightly lighted". Petersen's first bit of stage business, even as he is referring to the gossip-clouded relationship between Old Werle and Mrs. Sörby, is the lighting of a lamp and the replacing of its shade. The establishment of dialogue of themes of sexual adventuring and illicit enterprise is thus counterpointed by visual references to light and shadow and, by

11

implication, the difficulty of "seeing". This counterpoint runs through the play, though there is some interplay of function between what is seen and what is heard.

The less-obvious Christ-theme is established somewhat later on, though just as emphatically. Old Werle, who is crucially involved in the primary themes already described, points out in speaking for the first time that the dinner party has constituted "thirteen at table", something considered ominous. And with a nod he indicates that his son's guest, Hjalmar, is the unusual thirteenth (p. 108). This social brutishness on Werle's part quite naturally makes Hjalmar uncomfortable and ready to leave; and when he talks of the situation later (p. 128), he is careful to give only an approximate number of guests, "twelve or fourteen", thus avoiding the unlucky reality. But it is Gregers who decides himself to be life's thirteenth-at-table, and his statement to this effect, abruptly countered by Relling, forms the basis for the play's final exchange of dialogue. So that whether or not it can be shown that Ibsen's use of a Christ-motif was fully conscious, their positions of emphasis make the references to this notion of "thirteenth at table" worth our noticing.

Now this superstition against having thirteen at table obviously stems from something more significant than the social nicety of wishing to see each guest effectively partnered: the precedent of the Last Supper, at which Christ sat down with the Twelve, an event ending in betrayal and death. In other words, a dinner for thirteen implies that someone is fated to play Jesus, and someone else Judas. To be thirteenth a table, therefore, can be said to appeal to the paranoiac in us all, for the saving grace of paranoia is that it reassures us that *someone* cares; the odd thirteenth—however determined—can always tell himself that he is therefore special, a fated victim. No one, of course, would imagine himself a Judas, but many would play the Christ. In Ibsen's play, Old Werle makes it possible for both "thirteenths", Gregers and Hjalmar, to thus single themselves out; both of them would-be transcendental personalities with eyes upon the Ideal, they are presumably purer and more spiritual than other men: in short, Christs. In point of fact, each man is later shown to be a betrayer, helping to lead at least one other to sorrow and to death. Moreover, if in the drama of the

New Testament someone "must" play the role of Judas, Relling is right in pointing out that no one is forced to do so in life. "Thirteenth at table" is simply one more delusion in a play full of illusory activity.

The enormous number of instances of reference to sight, already referred to, reinforce the theme of self-delusion—and, of course, the deluding of others. Old Werle had hinted to Hjalmar that Gregers was angry with him, Hjalmar, and had led the latter into his career in photography (p. 109).[2] Gregers wonders whether his father has not been so kind to Hjalmar in order "to atone for something" (p. 110), which leads immediately into a presentation of the Gina-Hjalmar marriage and its attendant mysteries. Indeed, Gregers goes on, Old Werle "seems to have played the part of Divine Providence" towards Hjalmar (p. 112). Here we are dealing with a playwright much interested in father-son bonds, especially those involving godlike fathers and sacrificial sons; this particular father has bad eyes, and cannot abide smoking in his "sanctum" (p. 112). Werle reacts with displeasure at the sight of Old Ekdal, his former partner, but in a scene reminiscent of Peter's denial of Christ, Hjalmar refuses to "see" his father as he passes (p. 115).

Clearly, the roles of victim and victimizer are going to be juggled in this play. Old Werle now tells his son that Old Ekdal is the sort who will "dive straight to the bottom and never come up again"—exactly the description, put positively, later used to explain the nobility of the wild duck. This is, in fact, the first appearance of the wild duck theme in the play, but it obviously augments the others and, in a sense, connects them. The duck, a sacrificial animal no less than the traditional lamb, is distinguished by being unwilling to live crippled or consciously unfree: it would rather die. Thus the duck becomes the emblem of a special sort of Christ.

Werle confirms the fact of his weakening eyes and offers his son a partnership that would, in effect, mean an exchange of their previous roles; but in a recounting of the history of their unhappy family, the son refuses (pp. 120-22). Old Ekdal accuses his son of looking at things "through your mother's eyes", eyes which were frequently "clouded"—blurred by alcohol, apparently; but the son counters by blaming the father for the mother's condition (pp. 122-23). The first act ends, we notice, with the guests playing a game with Mrs. Sörby; do we need to be told that it is a game of Blindman's Buff (p. 123)?

Act II begins with the same unremitting emphasis upon vision. We are in a photographic studio, and a lamp, window, and shade are conspicuous; reading and sewing are going on, and shortly Hedwig will begin to draw (pp. 124-25). Grandfather, Old Ekdal, returns from the Werles' with copying work to do—and the present of a bottle of brandy (p. 126; soon there will be beer as well). While it is not quite a stone that he gives her to eat, Hjalmar does perform the cruelty of handing Hedwig, whom he has promised an enjoyable snack from the dinner party, a menu to read instead (pp. 131-32). He does not mean to be cruel; he is simply and stupidly selfish. But his behaviour is solidly founded on a self-deluding quality, the habit of convincing himself that his is a noble mind forced to live amid squalid conditions—though it will eventually produce something very fine. (A regular Christian martyr, as Amanda in *The Glass Menagerie* would say.) Hedwig's eye-weakness is leading to blindness, and is probably hereditary (p. 135). Naturally, it does not take Gregers long to deduce the truth about Hedwig's parentage and the circumstances surrounding Gina's wedding to Hjalmar.

Old Ekdal, a mighty hunter in his time, now does his hunting in the attic, as we are about to learn; but the notion of hunting in the play becomes, eventually, a euphemism for male sporting with womankind. Thus a line such as Old Ekdal's "The forest takes revenge, you see" is bound to sound ominously prophetic (p. 138). It expresses the notion of an outraged Nature demanding its revenge, its satisfaction for unnatural actions. Here are little men talking mightily about "the Ideal" in a situation where the natural law itself is being violated. One might as well attempt to imprison the forest itself in an attic—and to that we are now introduced (pp. 138-40). The prize specimen this attic preserves, a bird no less important than Chekhov's seagull and far overshadowing Miss Julie's greenfinch, is of course the wild duck. It bears a wound from which it tried to take refuge in death. Old Werle's dog had dived down to save the duck, leaving its mark upon its body; but then, it was Old Werle who shot the duck in the first place (pp.

14

140-41).

The second act is ready to conclude, once we are given mention of the last characters we will need. There is the tippling ex-clergyman Molvik and the doctor Relling—more obscured vision, and in the latter instance occurring in a character who in Ibsen must be expected to provide a clear vision of the truth: a scientist. But the act does not end before Gregers expresses the wish to be himself the sort of "clever dog" that dives down to save suicidal ducks from dying (p. 143). Of course, he ignores the fact that in so doing, he thwarts their wishes and condemns them to imprisonment in an impaired state, even wounding them further in the process.

In the next act, it is daylight, and a reluctant Hjalmar is seen retouching photographs—falsifying a supposed idealization, in other words (p. 146). The new lodger, Gregers, has already disturbed and befouled the house by creating smoke, smell, and a swampy floor—much as he will shortly damage its resident family. We see that both Ekdal and Hjalmar are lazy workers who would rather be doing something else, something related to Nature, for example. But both of them have jobs to do, tasks involving close eye-work (pp. 147-48), though Hjalmar soon allows Hedwig to take over his work—salving his conscience by warning her that she does it "on [her] own responsibility" (p. 150).

As for Hedwig, she would cheerfully—as she confesses to Gregers—spend all her spare time in the attic, apparently because it acts as a spur to her imagination. There is a stopped clock in there, so that, as Gregers phrases it, "Time has ceased to exist in the wild duck's world." There are also books, with wonderful pictures of strange places, people, and periods. But one picture does show an unsettling image of a woman with Death and an hourglass! Hedwig does not expect to travel on her own, but rather to stay home and help her parents; yet if she could, she would like to create pictures too (pp. 151-53). Here, Ibsen cleverly presents Hedwig's secret world of the imagination, and establishes its connections with art, time, and Nature. With Gregers prompting her, Hedwig reveals that she thinks of the attic as "the boundless deep", an image reminiscent of the watery grave from which the duck was once pulled back; it is *her* duck, after all, though perhaps the place in

15

which it lives is not just an attic (pp. 153-54). By extending the parallels thus offered us, we can see the world of the attic as an attractive escape into death, one for which Hedwig may be secretly longing without being aware of the fact.

But attics can also be, as this one is, places where other sorts of imaginative enterprise are carried out; the Ekdals, father and son, hunt there. Gina agrees that men must do so, though of course Old Ekdal's rifle won't fire (p. 156). As for Hjalmar, he wants to combine science and art in his invention, whatever it may be; it is his "sacred duty" (p. 157). But whatever Ibsen might think of the fated enterprise of attempting to join reason and the imagination in such a way, it is clear that neither Ekdal has been able to use the pistol to take his life, and thus obliterate their failures (p. 158). Both men, of course, would wish it to be known that they had heroically looked the chance of death straight int he eye; but more important than any speculation about the pistol or Hjalmar's invention is the admission by Gregers that he thinks Hjalmar and the wild duck "have a lot in common" (p. 160). Gregers goes on talking of the swamps and poisons which this supposed wild duck has had to deal with, quite missing the point that Hjalmar has hardly had to deal with any reality whatsoever. The identity of Ibsen's wild duck figure is bandied about in the play as is that of Chekhov's seagull, but in both works significant mistakes are made by characters who cannot admit the truth until too late, if ever.

When Gregers meets Molvik and Relling (he knew Relling previously), he remarks that he might have need of their services because they had been "thirteen at table yesterday" (p. 161). Gregers here lays his sense of being fated before the feet of science and religion, though neither of the others can do much for him: Relling is suspicious, Molvik "daemonic", and Gregers' complaint patently absurd. Relling remembers Gregers for his having preached the Claim of the Ideal from house to house in Höjdal (p. 162). This exchange leads to an argument as to who is responsible for the "stench" said to pervade the Ekdal household (p. 164). The stench is claimed to have been caused by the "sick conscience" that Gregers admits he inherited from his mother; at least, he does not dispute his father's charge that such is true, though he would of course dispute the locus of ultimate blame (p. 166). In Relling's

16

phrase, Gregers has the "national disease", "integrity fever" (p. 168). All this, of course, is a way of making the specific general: of making Gregers' ailment, his mistaken pursuit of the Ideal, into a common Norwegian complaint. Referring backwards, Gregers' disease relates to its symptom, the stench, and through it to the swamp which is its origin; referring forwards, it strikes down the wild duck, which will not live amid miasma, and which would rather die than live unfree.

All this time, the Christ-theme is waiting for renewal. When Act IV begins, it is after great amounts of offstage action have taken place: that is, Gregers has revealed some of the truth to Hjalmar during their between-act walk together. When the onstge action resumes, Hjalmar is promising not to harm "a hair of [the wild duck's] head", though with a better sense of metaphor he would also like to "wring its neck"— thanks to the obligation thrust upon him by the "laws of the Ideal" (p. 171). Because it is time for honesty, Hjalmar shouts, "Light the lamp!" (p. 172); but candour is not to be achieved so easily. Gina reminds her husband that he had had "some pretty wild habits" before their marriage, but he counters with accusations that their household has become a "swamp of deceit" (p. 174). This mutual blaming is not of course what Gregers had anticipated, a Hjalmar "radiant—transfigured" (p. 176). There is more fussing about with lamp shades, and Gregers tells Hjalmar that "There's a lot of the wild duck in you"; but by this time, the analogy is hard to comprehend (p. 176). Only Relling is sensible enough to warn Hjalmar about the possible effect of all this upon his daughter—who is, after all, at a "difficult age" (pp. 177-78). Ibsen is setting up his martyr-figure within an ironic atmosphere of incipient adulthood: few of the supposed adults on stage recognize the fact of Hedwig's continuing maturation.

Mrs. Sörby enters—another understanding female, one who speaks of Werle's confidence in her, and of his developing blindness (pp. 180-81). Their coming marriage challenges Hjalmar's belief in "Divine Power", though Werle's failing eyesight does restore somewhat his sense of "Divine Justice" (p. 183). More to the point is Werle's bequest to Hedwig of a hundred crowns a month: Hjalmar exlaims, "The eyes! The eyes—and now, *this!*" (p. 185); Hjalmar decides that it is on

17

account of those eyes that he cannot bear to remain in his own home any longer (p. 187). His outburst is well understood by Gina, who admits that Gregers "meant it all for the best", but prays 'God forgive you all the same" (p. 188). Hedwig comprehends the similarities between herself and the wild duck, for both have entered the house "as a present", and so she is willing to listen to Gregers as he places in her mind the notion of sacrificing the wild duck for her father's sake (pp. 189-90). Then Act IV ends, on a note of turbulent emotion, with Gregers, Gina, and Hedwig all wondering how to bring Hjalmar home again, to stay.

With Act V under way, Ibsen can return his audience to some awareness of the Christ-motif; typically, he helps the process along with pieces of delayed exposition, however much they may be said to "pad" the play. We learn that Hjalmar had been considered a "shining light" by the two "soul-mothers"—his maiden aunts—who had raised him (p. 193). Relling adds a description of Gregers as "blind" and "sick" both—of "Integrity-Fever" and "hero worship" (p. 194). He himself can cope with such instances only by advocating the retention of the "Basic" or "Life-lie". Molvik and Old Ekdal are both examples of the efficacy of Relling's prescription, the good doctor carefully discriminating between his "Basic Lie" and the "lies" that are all Gregers' "ideals" amount to (p. 195). This confusion of lies and ideals produces the "fever" that now has Hjalmar in its grip.

Yet Gregers is undeterred: when Relling makes the dramatically convenient mistake of leaving him alone with Hedwig, Gregers again urges her to overcome her reluctance, a reluctance which is in effect her own good sense at work:

> GREGERS: If only your eyes had been opened to the true values in life; if you only had the joyous, courageous spirit of self-sacrifice, you'd see how quickly your father would come back to you—But I still have faith in you, Hedwig—don't forget that.
>
> (p. 196)

Hedwig has thus been given exactly the proper motivation for sacrifice, the one she is defenseless against: her need to earn back her father's love. The little godling brought up in the absence of a male principle to be a source of pure light in the

18

world is going to require a renewing sacrifice. Within seconds, Hedwig is wondering how one goes about killing wild ducks, handling the double-barreled pistol ominously.

When Hjalmar returns, muttering darkly about there being an "intruder" about, Hedwig is "confused and terrified"—and she is only able to resume control over her emotions by stating purposefully, "The wild duck!" (pp. 199-200). This is a moment of crucial decision-making for any company choosing to put on the play. If Hedwig is shown as clearly determined upon her own death at this early point, then presumably the audience will suffer enormously during the next few pages of dialogue, however much it will listen to what is actually being said. More appropriately, Hedwig should be played as giving away nothing more definite than an intention to consider killing her duck, as Gregers has asked. The identification of herself with the wild duck, clear enough in retrospect (whatever Gregers has to say on the subject), should come about by means of her suicidal act, and that act itself must result from the conversation she now overhears, most of it in the form of disclosures made by Hjalmar.

For the latter now reveals that Hedwig's faith in his invention (leaving aside the question of its practicality) has been of primary importance to his happiness. Despite the fact that his happiness is equivalent to ignorance of certain truths, Hjalmar makes Hedwig's withdrawal of faith the cause of his life now being plunged "into darkness" (p. 204). "To see her blinking up at me with those sweet little eyes of hers so full of happiness", he continues with unwitting cruelty, was what kept faith in himself alive; now it is gone. As figure of Christ, Hedwig rekindles a faith in the self which has been defined in terms of light, but which is surely illusory; in a sense, either her mission must be said to fail or it is to be executed in a context of dramatic irony that undercuts the value of all human undertakings of this "role". Hedwig is to play the part which Eugene O'Neill will later give to Hickey's wife and Arthur Miller to Linda Loman: faithful believer in the dreaming of an undeserving male. But whereas Hickey will kill his too-believing wife, and Willie get free of Linda only by killing himself, Hedwig is being urged towards self-sacrifice by false-Christs, or false prophets. Gregers, who is illuminated by a spurious Ideal, and Hjalmar, who is used to the support of believing ladies, are about to bring about Hedwig's taking her life for Hjalmar's sake.

For he has had his eyes "opened", and whereas he once thought that his greatest joy would have been "to take her hand and lead her through life, as one might lead a frightened child through a dark, empty room", now he can no longer assume that she would readily choose him instead of the chance of a "better life". How cruelly Hjalmar states his own reliance on his daughter's destruction: the question is unbearable for Hedwig, and a shot is immediately heard. Gregers, who thinks he understands what has happened, shouts out in joy (p. 206). It's the wild duck, he says, "the thing she loved best in the world"—and it has been sacrificed for her father. But she loved her father even better: her "greater" love meets the Christian specification exactly. When the deed is discovered, each person reacts according to his limitations of perception—Old Ekdal muttering about the revenge of the forest, Molvik quoting his Biblical phrases, Hjalmar thinking only of his lost opportunities (pp. 208-9). But though Molvik assures us that "The child is not dead; it sleepeth", there will be no miracle, for a misunderstood gesture cannot redeem a single human soul. Nothing "noble" of Hjalmar will persist, Relling says, and we must believe him.

Another "thirteenth at table" has created another Jesus: that is, another betrayal of a saving spirit has occurred because of another commitment to a misplaced Ideal. But to Gregers' reassertion of his destiny as fated thirteenth, Relling's response is an abrupt "The Hell it is" (p. 210). Ibsen gives the last word to the character who sees the danger in false ideals, and who ironically preaches the need for redemptive self-deception. But nothing good will come of the pursuit of the false Ideal by inferior men. If Hedwig dies, essentially, to accomplish the completion of Hjalmar as a person, then her effort is in vain. *The Wild Duck* chronicles the establishment in modern drama of one of its abiding themes, the disparity between illusion and reality, and the subjective nature of their interreaction, as imaged forth in terms of vision. As the effect of cumulative guilt darkens the physical vision, metaphysical sight is also jeopardized by insufficiency of personal integrity. It is a tragic and vicious circle which perpetually besets our modern theatre.

When our prophets fail, we do not lack for Christs; but the closed heart admits of no salvation. Or can we find ourselves again: let the wild duck fly free?

NOTES

1 Henrik Ibsen, *The Wild Duck*, in *The Wild Duck and Other Plays*, trans. Eva Le Gallienne (New York, 1961). All page references appear parenthetically within my text.
2 The visual media referred to in *The Wild Duck* rival, in number and scope, the communications media represented in Ingmar Bergman's film *The Silence*.

2

Strindberg's Paranoid Christ: *The Father*

They Are (she is) Out To Get Him—indeed, with success; but the complicity of the protagonist is what makes the downfall interesting. In August Strindberg's 1882 play *The Father*,[1] the insecurities of the author are projected upon the play's title-character in ways which, though fascinating, are beyond our capacities to assess fully. What remains that *is* of literary importance, however, is the way in which Captain Adolf's downfall, so clearly assisted by his own refusals to make the adjustments his intelligence should be able to suggest to him, creates in the audience a tension which is never finally erased by explanation; in other words, *The Father*'s dramatic success rests largely upon the ambiguity caused by overlapping responsibilities: the Captain's culpability begins long before his wife Laura's malice has fully exerted itself. What explains this redundancy of causality, if not the muddle of the author's own mental state? The Captain's adoption of the role of irreligious Christ does, I think, provide us with an exposition of the dramatic core of *The Father*, one which is finally both of demonstrable pertinence and of critical value.

What does the modern audience make of the trappings of *The Father*'s opening Act? For the revelations that take place in Act II, which include the Captain's feelings of having been an unwanted child, his playing the boy in the presence of his wife, and his not being "allowed to" take part in the war (p. 47), all make pathetic exposition of the leather gear that surrounds the Captain throughout the play, but which is brought to the

22

audience's attention during the initial stage-directions: guns and military coats, and even leather upholstery on the couch (p. 15). What can we think—indeed, what can Strindberg's first audience have thought—of this swaggering masculinity, and whose insecurities is this display meant to bolster? Though the play specifically opposes the military to the divine (p. 16), a surrogate belief is nevertheless being established here—one which reaches its final dramatic epitome with the Captain spread like butchered meat—or the crucified Christ—across the pitying arms of his attendant females.

What I am claiming is that whatever Strindberg thought of *The Father* as a presentation of the tragedy of pride—a telling loss in the life of an otherwise admirable figure—his play is instead a no less affecting drama of personal surrender. The situation is one in which the Woman finally advances to occupy a territory which the Man has long since ceded, in effect, because that masculine agent had come to rely not upon its own inherent worthiness, but upon the legalistic buttressing of a sexist civil law. And it seems highly ironic that Captain Adolf, who rejects the pastor's Christian admonition not to judge (in the case of the erring Nöjd) and complains of the sectarian tug-of-war going on in his household over the person of his daughter Bertha (p. 18), becomes himself exactly what he seems to boast of not being: "neither a witness to the truth nor a martyr" (p.21). This Captain has long been ready to climb upon the nearest cross, as soon as one is proffered.

For the Captain is, as Strindberg presents him, quite apt to think of his wife as a kind of whore; he hands over her household funds at the same time as they discuss the mutual roles of husband and wife in the upbringing of a child:

> CAPTAIN: Children are to be brought up in their father's faith, according to the law.
> LAURA: And their mother has nothing to say about it.
> CAPTAIN: Nothing at all! She sold her birthright and gave up her rights in return for her husband's assuming responsibility for her and her children.
> LAURA: So a mother has no rights over the child?
> CAPTAIN: None at all! If you've sold something, you're not likely to get it back and keep the money, too.   (p. 22)

This exchange, which leaves Laura looking at the money in her hand as dramatic correlative of the hard lesson she has just been taught (p. 23), amounts to a cash haggling over the value of parenthood; it reduces the Captain's subsequent discussion with the Doctor of things spiritual by its ugly materialism.

The Captain's objection to the Doctor's lackadaisical acceptance of whatever accommodations come his way is an angry "For Christ's sake . . ." (p. 27). But his commitment to blunt partisanship in the matter of his daughter's care is equally strenuous: "I want to give her my soul, too" (p. 28). We are looking at the actions and statements of a man who can describe Margret's faith—her "true faith"—as one of "hate", yet warns her in terms she can understand that if she deserts him, she is "committing a sin" (p. 29). In other words this renegade from the Christian community is reserving for himself the right to play the role of condemned and unresurrectable Christ, if and when the mood suits him to do so. Whoever is not with the Captain, it seems, is against him—a description classic in its quality of paranoia (for anyone not truly divine, that is).

Just as it is difficult to ignore the implications of the Captain's description of Laura's power as "satanic" (p. 32), we may give corresponding figurative weight to the Nurse's curtain line for Act One: "Jesus, help us! What's going to happen now?" (p. 34); the Ibsenian melodrama of the question implies a serious invocation of *some* Jesus or other. While such references are not always to be given full metaphoric credit, they must at least be accepted as helping create a resonance of interpretive possiblity, a poetic space to sound about in. Given the whining quality of the presentation of "suffering" evident in Strindberg's fiction, moreover, we are perhaps that much the readier for the Captain's responding to normal feminine fussiness as some of the slings and arrows of outrageous fortune, or as the nibbling away by little enemies at the person of the Overman. Domestic silliness—the treating as a small boy of a man who had never felt wanted as a child, and who never completely grew up thereafter—is meant to support a near-Shakespearean isolation of a tragic hero, at least throughout its early stages.

That isolation, aggravated by the Strindbergian red herring of the eternal doubt about the real paternity of their children supposedly common to all fathers—hardly enough, therefore, to establish the Captain's dramatic uniqueness—seems underscored by a number of resemblances between the Captain's plight and those of certain Shakespearean protagonists, especially in terms of their degree of aloneness. With a certain elasticity in applying the parallel, we may note that the Captain resembles the following: Lear in his habit of making gruff blind demands on the loyalty of his women; Caesar in his unwillingness to credit feminine intuition as against the callings of his own vanity; Hamlet in his indecisiveness; Othello in his raging jealousy and his recourse to animal imagery for sex; Richard II in the pathos of his faith in the integrity of his role; Richard III in his spiritual crippledom; Shylock in his sense of being persecuted because he is only a man (his parody of Shylock's speech, in Act II [p. 46], is a remarkable display of self-pity). But most importantly and finally, he has a Lady Macbeth wife; the parallels here are too many to ignore and yet the Captain's complicity in his own downfall threatens to blind us to the extremity of Laura's machinations.

Of course, there are other literary references to extend the allusive richness of the Captain's role. Allusions are made to Oedipus, to Hercules, and to the husband of Mrs. Alving in Ibsen's *Ghosts*. Incredibly, both the Captain and the Doctor join in wishing that Alving had had the chance to speak in his own defence (p. 41). Strindberg's open and sneering attack on Ibsen's feminism merely confirms what the substance of the play and its presentation of character make patent enough; and the depiction by Strindberg of a Christ of masculinity creates a less than accidental parallel with the Christ-figures I have chosen to represent playwrights whose philosophical tenents are not wholly dissimilar to Strindberg's: Ibsen and Shaw. Both men identified their Christness with at least symbolic femaleness, while Strindberg's posture—as noted in his reference to Ibsen—is revealingly close to the Captain's attitude.

Such literary extensions of the Captain, moreover, are apparently intended to heighten the tragic stature of a character who is not only proud, but also heedless, petulant, childish, and sexually biased. Nothing in this lessens the pathos of the play's closing moments, perhaps; but those do not embody tragic grandeur. Consciously or not, Strindberg gives us a character of somewhat fragile masculinity, who is beset by a female with a genuine grievance to express. If the Captain's suffering is beyond his deserving, it is also augmented by his participation in his own undoing. Though the direct religious expression in the play is of the servant-class pietistic kind we recognize from *Miss Julie,* still the sexual savagery falls short of the warfare in *The Dance of Death* (which poor direction can turn ludicrous). The real distinction between this play and Strindberg's other works is provided by the intended Christ-parallel, and it is the latter presence that provides the play with its distinctive qualities of literary resonance—and not its equipment of occasional allusions to other literature.

The Captain imagines himself the noble Roman, for whom, as a man, "the only thing I can do is to cross my arms on my chest like the Romans and hold my breath until I die" (p. 41). What is being foreshadowed here is, of course, the Captain's straitjacketing later in the play, and his sensation of being suffocated—by womb-return, as it were. What Strindberg may not have perceived in this linking of Roman manhood and suffocated infant is its middle state: the spoiled child holding its breath until it gets its way. Moreover, because the Captain has no faith in an afterlife, he can only believe in the form of immortality provided by the daughter he is shortly to lose—a loss which, in effect, guarantees his total effacement from the earth (p. 44). Yet the true parallel is not with noble Romans but rather—as if by way of parody—to crucified Jews. Though he has not yet extended his arms as if for the nails, the Captain's imagined crossing of arms befits his inbound mental state, and promises the tomb. Wanting a mother, he could yet have been Laura's friend in his helplessness; needing a wife, he became her enemy. Though the discussion between husband and wife in Act II polarizes their conflict, the dramatic process involved is more like a chemical reaction in which a stronger agent deprives a weaker of its surrounding particles.

The Captain and Laura reach a peak of malice, during this frank exchange of verbal viciousness (at which Strindberg is a master), with the curtain moment of violence that ends Act II: the Captain throwing his lighted lamp at the woman who has just discarded him (p. 48). As he recognizes his coming abandonment, a discarded state like that of the black widow's mate, the Captain's furious gesture provides what could be said to empasize further the parallel between the Captain and the suffering Jesus. Especially to an audience in a Lutheran country, the Captain's frenzied exasperation as he flings the lamp at Laura should recall, at least subconsciously, the famous incident in which Luther threw his inkpot at the devil. For the Captain even calls Laura (depending on the translation) "demonic" or "satanic", and his act is a justified rage against a party whose incredible perfidy has just been revealed. (Within the career of the Biblical Jesus, the cleansing of the temple is perhaps the only pertinent parallel of righteous anger.) Because the Captain imagines that he talks sweet reason with his wife— an aspect of that scientific intelligence he possesses, and that the play shows her incapable of fathoming—his action here is nothing less than the measure of the sudden discovered gulf between his rational fairness and his wife's instinctive recourse to foul play. And yet, we remember, the man is also clearly going mad, even as he is being outplotted by his supposedly unintelligent, instinctual wife.

In Act III, once Laura's half-brother the Pastor admits thinking of the Captain, "that freethinker", as rather "a weed in our garden" (p. 51), the Captain's encirclement by his enemies is completed. He enters with an armload of books, all of them full of references to deceived husbands and intriguing wives, and speaks wildly about Irishmen throwing lamps at their wives. His discourse possesses the raging quality of sundered selfhood that we may note in the final speeches of Othello. What is more, he moves suddenly from a defence of lamp-throwing to a complex discussion of "belief" in more than one sense:

> CAPTAIN: Nothing! A man never knows anything; he only believes. Isn't that right, Jonas? If you believe, you're saved! Yes, that one would be! No, I know one can be damned because of his faith. I know!
>
> (p. 54)

In these lines (rather woodenly translated, from the actor's point of view), the Captain makes the connection between religious belief, by which, in a Protestant interpretation, one can be "saved" without having to act, and the trusting of wives by their husbands. The imposition of religious upon sexual meanings is especially telling because the Captain, "that freethinker", has learned through bitter experience that his substitute religion—the one through which his posterity, his immortality, could have been assured—has instead damned him to the clutches of his personal devil. His "hope for eternal life" taken away (p. 55), the Captain is left with nothing but a despairing knowledge.

More awesome still is the Captain's exchange with his daughter, whom he has already—and needlessly—frightened into the enemy camp. He tells Bertha—who only wants to be herself, and not the battleground of her father's and mother's souls—that he is a "cannibal", and wants to "eat" her up (p. 56). This favourite Strindberg metaphor, tellingly borrowed perhaps from half-remembered fairy-tales, is used by the Captain to extend the oedipal struggle to fathers and daughters, presumably because the latter are tainted by the presence in them of the mother-soul. He wishes to shoot the child (cf. *The Wild Duck*), because it has lately bared its teeth at him; the irony of this development lies in the maddened Captain's willingness to commit a sort of self-suicide (as he has in effect himself defined it) by devouring his daughter before she devours him. The effect of marriage is thus a destruction of belief, and the Captain's state is the insanity of psychic despair:

> CAPTAIN: Why didn't you let me kill the child? Life is hell, and death is heaven, and children belong to heaven!
> NURSE: What do you know about what comes after death?
> CAPTAIN: That's the only thing one knows, but about life one knows nothing! If one had only known that from the beginning.
> (p. 58)

One suspects that in this maddened Lear's insights are hidden the innermost secrets of August Strindberg himself, and that they centre around the discovery of an existential hell, for which marriage and childbearing are only convenient metaphors, and not in fact the actual "subjects" of *The Father*. At any rate, they have led him to the expression of one of modern theatre's commonest "truths", that death is all we shall know of bliss.

And yet the implied ability to re-envelop the child, or the

child-man, is physiologically and psychologically the province of womankind, protected as they are by the mystique of apparent helplessness. When the Captain calls Nöjd to help him escape the psalm-reading Nurse, who has just straitjacketed him, Nöjd refuses—saying that "there's something special so a man doesn't want to lay a hand on a woman", for "It's like religion" (p. 58). The Captain blames it all on modern "spiritual marriage", which has taken away "good, healthy, sensual love" (p. 59), and goes on to ask the Albeesque question, "Who is the physical father of the spiritual child?" Nobody wanted what has come to pass, it seems; but how, then, has it occurred?

> CAPTAIN: . . . Who rules over life, then?
> LAURA: God alone does . . .
> CAPTAIN: The god of strife then. Or the goddess nowadays! . . .
> (p. 60)

And so we have the identification of sexual insurrection and conventional religiosity in the person of a malign female deity. Strindberg has encapsuled all his favourite villainies in a single dramatic epiphany, and now the Captain is ready for his crippling stroke, for probable silence, and for an ironic second infancy.

But not before the creation of an affecting final tableau in which the Captain sinks his head into the lap of the Nurse, asking her to bend over him so that he can feel the comforting presence of her breasts—this from the man who has just complained of the suffocating "cat" (the Nurse's shawl) which has been thrown over him; perhaps this Cyrano-like concern for appearances is the Captain's closest approach to tragic stature, for in demanding that the shawl be replaced with his tunic, his "tough lion's skin", the Captain resumes some pathetic vestige of control over his "equipment" (p. 60). Yet in preparing himself for his final dramatic moment, a stasis of symbolic meaning, the Captain has also returned to the dependence upon an outer show of strength, on the associations of dress, that characterized his first appearance in the play.

This final vision is, moreover, deliberately pathetic, for in surrounding him with women, having him lie across the lap of the most maternal one, and adding the presence, at the last, of the symbolic representatives of Science and Religion,

29

Strindberg lends his creature the status of a Christ just taken down from the cross, a figure in a painter's *Pietà*. What follows is quite consciously Biblical in tone and effect, and cannot help remind the audience of what the playwright wishes them to feel—the turning, at the end, of modern Man into the very things he said he would not be: witness to the truth, and martyr.

Consider the allusive sequence of this conclusion to the play: in place of Christ's exchange with Mary and John, we get Laura's offer to let the Captain see Bertha, followed by Adolf's cynical statement that "A man has no children", only women do, so "the future is theirs". The Captain's sighing the opening of a prayer, "Oh, God who loves children!", is taken to be a prayer by the Nurse, who draws the attention of the others to it in language reminiscent of Matthew 27:47, where Jesus's cry of momentary near-despair is misinterpreted as a call to Elias; similarly, the Nurse distorts the Captain's final call into what it most surely is not—a confession of faith. Wearily, the Captain tells Margret "Good night", then adds the parodic ". . . and blessed be you among women!"—unnoticed by his attendants. Whether he still breathes or has died is briefly debated, while Science and Religion quarrel about meanings; and the Doctor issues the Biblical-sounding injunction, "Let him who knows more speak!" And as Mother and Child embrace in new harmony (achieved cruelly at the expense of the recumbent Captain), the Pastor pronounces his blessing: "Amen!" (pp. 61-2).

It is a powerful ending, but one which—in its parody of not only the Bible but also Ibsen's *Ghosts*—has an unsettling effect upon the audience far beyond its apparent means. Brief and intense, *The Father* is a play which teaches us that Life is a game in which advancement is impossible by reason of the game's own blind priorities, its jungle norms. If it is not perhaps the tragedy of a single man at all, but rather the study of paranoia ending in pathos, still it underscores a perversely cynical view of history— one in which the rule of the Father-God is reversed and the days of the Great Mother return—and with a vengeance. Creator and destroyer (Kali, Ishtar, or however named), she reconfirms the Manichaean view of things at best, and at the worse presents all mankind as being on the Cross. More clearly than most modern playwrights, the unbeliever Strindberg has etched the figure of a Christ into our dramatic consciousnesses.

NOTES

1   August Strindberg, *The Father*, in *Pre-Inferno Plays*, trans. Walter Johnson (New York, 1976). All page references appear parenthetically within my text.

3

Shaw's Transfigured Christ: *Major Barbara*

One of the most fascinating of the several avatars of Christ in modern drama is Shaw's Major Barbara, for the play which bears her name (1905)[1] is not merely the "ethical discussion" which its author half-humorously called it (p. 186), but rests as drama upon underpinnings of myth both Christian and pagan. These underpinnings—these Greek and Christian references— are so complicatedly interwoven that it is difficult to argue just how much the author meant merely to suggest—or whether he saw limitations for his mythic parallels at all. So much is explicit, so much implied and expressed in the very name, that the close reader is encouraged to go on disovering by the very multiplicity of his discoveries. For instance, much of what is to follow depends upon associations between the name and character of Barbara and the myths of Christ and Dionysus; yet even a timid exploration of what her very name suggests yields not only the Dionysian sense of the wild, uncontrolled, *barbaric*, but also the fact that the Christian Saint Barbara, the victim of a fanatically pagan father, was delivered from his intentions by a timely bolt of lightning, and is therefore known as patroness of fireworks, arsenals, and artillery.

In my study of *Major Barbara*, minimum use will be made of Shaw's Prefaces and other prose—not only on the hackneyed but still valid grounds that the play must itself demonstrate (no mere statement of intent can establish by itself) but because Shaw is so careful to reintroduce, point by point, each element of his related prose argument within each play itself that the reader is seldom at a loss to find the one form of disclosure confirmed and clarified by the other. But I shall refer briefly to what Shaw says outside of the *Major Barbara* text, if only to confirm my interpretation of his sure and general intent.

To begin with, Shaw makes perfectly clear his contempt for conventional and institutional Christianity, particularly Christian morality—which he refers to as "our mercanto-Christian morality" (p. 20) and accepts "slave-morality" as a description of (p. 21). Within this frame of reference, he can term Undershaft his "hero" and contrast this hero with Peter Shirley—the "honest poor man" of the play—as a Dives contrasted with a Lazarus (p 27). (It is a contrast of an educational kind, especially when one considers that Undershaft is in partnership with one Lazarus.) Shaw goes on to defend his Barbara from objections to her despairing quotations of Christ (p. 136)—making in the process a definition of the sort of "divine" passion which he feels the theatre can, and should, possess (pp. 33-4). (The appropriate, and clever, response to this objection to Barbara's line appears later: pp. 191-93). Shaw seems fascinated by the strenuous nature of the Christianity of the organization he has chosen to present on stage—their substitution "of the drum for the organ", and all the militariness that this implies (p. 37). They would seem to represent a straining in the right direction, their "Blood and Fire" motto a considerable improvement over the abject timidity suggested by the Cross as conventionally interpreted.

Such conventional Christianity has made merit of "submission", and is itself "soul-destroying" and lacking in the "vitality" typical of the Salvation Army; the latter, with its Blood and Fire, themselves a wholesome change ("because fire is beautiful and blood a vital and splendid red"), banishes Fear, and thus "transfigured men and women carry their gospel through a transfigured world . . ." (pp. 39-40). It is the references to transfiguration by commitment to a vital cause that I especially wish to emphasize; indeed, Shaw specifically uses this key term. For although the Salvation Army has "too much other-worldliness" about it (p. 41), it does make possible a sort of visitation of divine afflatus, an ecstatic rising-up which reminds me of the Transfiguration scene in the New

Testament,[2] and which seems clearly intimated by Shaw's play's glorious climax of commitment.

For the rest, Shaw's quarrel with conventional and institutional Christianity is clearly defined. He objects to the central significance of the Cross ("which I loathe as I loathe all gibbets") but condones Christianity's "central truth . . . the vanity of revenge and punishment" (pp. 43-4). Barbara's actions, even while a member of the Salvation Army, distinguish her from conventional Christians, the members of what Shaw calls Crosstianity—that is, she already "imitates Christ" (p. 44). There is a "nobler and profounder Christianity which affirms the sacred mystery of Equality" (p. 56) and forbids vengeance; this is Barbara's sort, and it is significant that Shaw himself—in a press release he prepared himself— mentions with evident pleasure the memory of Salvation Army songs wherein the "drama of salvation was presented". Such presentations, which were to influence the later dramatist, brought the villains of the pieces to the point where their faces were "lighted with the light of Heaven" (pp. 194-95). It is this light which justifies Shaw's implied comparison of Barbara to Christ, and also answers the attacks upon her cry of Christ-resembling, apparent despair (pp. 191-93). We should look, then, for the process by which a girl who is already committed to a better sort of Christianity makes a further step, becoming even more Christlike in the process—becoming transfigured, transformed, by the light of her discovery of the life-force operating through her person.

Because *Major Barbara* depends for its dramatic structure upon a series of movements in quest of answers, and because it responds to scenic environments with appropriate changes of heart and statements of recognition, it is not surprising that the number of references to what I consider to be its Christ-motif increases as the play progresses, nor that we find rather few such references in those portions of the play that are dominated by the spirit of Crosstianity—that is, by Lady Britomart. Act I takes place in Lady Brit's library. Early on in her discussion of Undershaft with Stephen, mention is made of the firm's name, "Undershaft and Lazarus", and the fact that Stephen has been teased while at King's by "a little brute" for being the heir to a firm that could be subtitled "Death and Destruction Dealers:

address, Christendom and Judea" (p. 72). Presumably, Undershaft represents the "Christendom" factor here, for Lazurus seems, on other evidence in the play, to have confined himself to being the firm's external agent, and to arranging its financial dealings. Undershaft—address, Christendom—is interested primarily in manufacture. One is tempted, of course, to play with the name "Lazarus". It is surely intended to mean more than something suggestively Jewish, which in fact it is not. As in the case of John Arden's *Serjeant Musgrave's Dance*, I regard his naming as referring to the Lazarus who is not listened to, rather than the better-known one who rose from the dead.

The parody-Christianity of Undershaft, who is soon to be known as "Dionysus", is fascinating. He is, by reason of his firm's motto, "Unashamed" (p. 73); in other words, he practices what Lady Brit calls a "religion of wrongness": that is, he does the right things while preaching the wrong (in obvious distinction from conventional Christians, those who control the civilization his firm services) (p. 76). A foundling in a heritage of foundlings, he participates in a kind of tribal ritual whereby old kings are relaced by new. His presence is a constant reminder of older pagan forms, even as he parodies the appearance of the Redeemer on earth. Undershaft is quick to understand Barbara's belief in a Father who can take care of His children, and is ready to adopt her Army's motto of "Blood and Fire" (p. 88). The attraction of Undershaft and Barbara for one another depends upon their mutual understandings: on the one hand, they appreciate that morality must reserve a place for force, "cannons and torpedoes"; on the other, that all men are a curious admixture of good and evil, and that no party has a monopoly of goodness (p. 90). The Sword and the Cross are deliberately set at odds in mutual challenge, but in reality they ought to be partners in combat—as Shaw is clearly out to prove (p. 91).

To speculate on the meanings of names that are relevant to the argument: Barbara has already been referred to, both in the apparently-intended sense of "barbaric"—her name, and the Graeco-Roman term for stranger, having the same roots—and with reference to her function as Christian patroness (a curious anomaly if ever there was one—which must have fascinated Shaw). Undershaft suggests, of course, the daemonic; the tunneler-under. He undermines, even as he digs towards Light. In the latter sense, he is the benign devil, Lucifer, bearer of light—who befriends mankind by showing it the possibility of choice between good and evil. Thus Undershaft is a quaint combination of Prometheus and Dionysus, a mixture reconciled only within Shaw's Nietzschean philosophy. A properly Hegelian synthesis is in the works.

In Act II, we are within Barbara's world—the West Ham Salvation Army shelter. Words and deeds are immediately set in opposition by Jenny's simple charity and Barbara's admonition to pray (pp. 99-100). But Bill Walker's entrance puts Jenny's "God forgive you" in jeopardy (p. 101); clearly, there is more demanded of the Christian than forgiveness, and Peter Shirley's sturdy defiance seems to be quite appropriate (p. 102). This Christ-in-the-Temple righteous anger appears to earn Shaw's applause, and Barbara's brisk confidence in dealing with Bill (pp. 105-6), otherwise so admirable, may be seen as a way of preparing the audience for the argument between Shirley's traditional and unappealing secularism and Undershaft's redemptive diabolism: that is, his overturned Christianity (pp. 110-11). Of course, there is instant sympathy between Shirley and Undershaft, for philosophically, they are really quite near. We are given a convincing demonstration of the power of Barbara's thinking when Bill is broken down before our eyes (p. 113); the inclination of the latter, however, is strongly towards retributive violence (p. 114).

It is at this point in the play that Shaw allows his characters to enact his philosophical tenets. Cusins begins (p. 117) with an explanation of why he has affiliated himself with the Salvation Army, reasons which of course are concerned with the worship of Dionysus; he claims that, "money and guns" aside, happy living constitutes a "heaven". Undershaft reminds him of the need for money, and Cusins persists, reaching the height of his paean in a tribute to an Absolute to which he cleverly gives the name "Barbara". "And shall not Barbara be loved for ever?" he asks, adding that "It is a fair translation" because "The word means Loveliness". This is a monumental piece of word-play that is apt to be lost on most audiences; Shaw refers to the Greek *Tò kalón*, the beautiful, the noble (p. 118). In quoting Euripides, he invokes a classical exponent of the notion of the Life-Force:

specifically, *The Bacchae*. The text quoted is part of a choral utterance the opening lines of which Shaw no doubt balked at using in his 1905 play:

> When shall I dance once more
> with bare-feet the all-night dances,
> tossing my head for joy
> in the damp air, in the dew,
> as a running fawn might frisk
> for the green joy of the wide fields,
> free from fear of the hunt,
> free from the circling beaters
> and the nets of woven mesh
> and the hunters hallooing on
> their yelping packs? And then, hard pressed,
> she sprints with the quickness of wind,
> bounding over the marsh, leaping
> to frisk, leaping for joy,
> gay with the green of the leaves,
> to dance for joy in the forest,
> to dance where the darkness is deepest,
>   where no man is.[3]

This is the true Life-Force, the cause and source of Cusins' worship. In its Euripidean expression, the choral passage just completed, it contains the elements of pastoral ecstasy to which Barbara attains in the final moments of the play. Interesting, too, is the substitution of an escaping game animal, representing joyous freedom, for the conventional Crosstian sacrificial lamb, symbol of accepting meekness. For although the play is comedy—and although the ending is undercut by traditionally necessary good spirits—there is little chance of evading Shaw's serious and underlying purposes.

By substituting a name that denotes the idea of the "strange" and new, Cusins replaces the *notion* of the noble and beautiful in Euripides' text with a specific name, that of an identifiable *personage*, his Barbara. She is, though she does not know it as yet, the Life-Force embodied; she is the redemption of his quaint notions about the Beautiful and Noble. Though she is righteous about accepting money from inappropriate sources (pp. 123-24), she can approve the giving of such funds (in this latter instance, money from Bill Walker) to the likes of Rummy Mitchens (p. 127). Barbara's charity is thus protected by a

37

personal sense of decorum, the sense of appropriateness that a priestess might possess.

But affairs do not go well for Barbara later in this scene. Violence by the poor in pursuit of a worthwhile cause is approved of (p. 127), while Barbara's idealism is disparaged (p. 132). Cusins' identifying of Undershaft with Dionysus (p. 135) is almost simultaneous with Barbara's decision to leave the Army. Her despair (p. 136) is expressed in a pointed echo of Christ's words: "My God: why hast thou forsaken me?", while Cusins is jubilant at Undershaft's triumph. Certainly the action of the play is far removed from the final victory of the "free" spirit Barbara represents at this point; all she can do is unconfidently offer Peter Shirley charity—tea and a night's lodging (pp. 138-39). Undershaft has swept the field before him, and Act II ends with the play's "hero" having routed his nominal enemy on that enemy's home grounds.

And so Act III begins on a note of dramatic expectation: after this moment of apparent deprivation, can Barbara salvage faith in herself, and faith in what she holds sacred? Next day, she is seen out of uniform and in pain, and within Lady Brit's own precincts (p. 140). Yet almost immediately, the issues of the play are raised to a higher level: whether there are, as Barbara puts it, "larger loves and diviner dreams than the fireside ones" (p. 142). Cusins agrees that there is a "holier ground" on which he must be won over, if he is to be won over completely. Undershaft's power as "Prince of Darkness" is generally acknowledged, but what that power's final effect shall ultimately be is yet to be determined. Certainly the decision will not be made according to convention, for from what is expected Stephen would inherit the Undershaft firm; but as it is, he shall do no such thing (p. 145). The principle by which a deserving foundling shall inherit—a good socialistic solution Brecht would have approved of—is part of the play's call for revolutionary answers to radical problems. It seems that Lazarus has spoken with the voice of a prophet—or of heaven— and a choice must soon be made (p. 146). The act of freeing Barbara, freedom itself being freed, is either a form of dramatic time-marking or an integral part of the play's rhetorical movement.

That movement continues, and the scene ends, with

Undershaft's blistering attack upon conventional moral judgements and the pretensions upon which they are routinely made in our society (pp. 150-51). It is agreed that all will visit Undershaft's "death and devastation factory", though a moody Cusins—his temporary exaltation now quite departed—is seen to wonder, "Why are we two coming to this Works Department of Hell?" (pp. 153-54). But it is no "pit" of torment at all, Undershaft assures Barbara. And then, as if to promise her the restoration of her faith in herself, he convinces the despairing Barbara that the "soul" she had held in her hand the day before could not fail to have been influenced by her (pp. 154-56). Barbara's face immediately lights up with restored "happiness" and "faith"; Undershaft may be the "clever clever devil" Cusins calls him, but the voice of God may be speaking through him too, as even Barbara confesses (p. 156). Thus the integrity of one of its central characters is restored (somewhat glibly, perhaps) as the play enters its final scene. Indeed, that integrity has been restored for Cusins as well, if we read aright his exclamation to Barbara as he exits: "My guardian angel!" (p. 156). For though Cusins is prone to using Greek references (thanks to Shaw's clever choice of occupations for him), he is quick enough to recognize—simple praise of his beloved aside—what function Barbara would exercise within the Christian tradition; "angel", she is humankind on the way to transcending its own limitations, and attaining to Spirit.

Undershaft's community lacks only a cathedral, Cusins admits, "to be a heavenly city instead of a hellish one" (p. 158). Indeed, Perivale St. Andrews would seem to have been designed to resemble the City of God, if not its parody: "an almost smokeless town of white walls, roofs of narrow green slates or red tiles, tall trees, domes, campaniles, and slender chimney shafts, beautifully situated and beautiful in itself" (p. 157). With its domes and campaniles—yet coming as it does as a surprise to its new visitors, who might realistically be expected to have heard of the place and its wonders—this town which bears its owner's name must look, as it lies there spread out upon the backdrop, like a vision of unearthly splendour, the realization of a flight of fancy. We are reminded that *Major Barbara* is utopian literature; the town's name may even be translated as "around the valley (or, arguably, the fairy-valley) of the blessed manliness". What Cusins may debate the eschatological status of is, after all, merely the triumph of all that is best in the human spirit. It is a vision meant to seduce.

And seduce it does. Cusins reveals that his love for Barbara has set him free from the need to cater to "the approval of [his] conscience" (p. 163). And now he has no need whatever for such conventional posturings:

> CUSINS: It is true. You accused me yourself, Lady Brit, of joining the Army to worship Barbara; and so I did. She bought my soul like a flower at a street corner; but she bought it for herself.
> UNDERSHAFT: What! Not for Dionysus or another?
> CUSINS: Dionysus and all the others are in herself. I adored what was divine in her, and was therefore a true worshipper ...   (p. 164)

Thus Barbara, for Cusins, embodies all that is "divine" to his way of thinking, and is therefore indeed the god-woman who will work his redemption. Whereas once Cusins was merely "romantic" about her, now he has been freed by the truth; among the specific truths he cites is the fact that "her father was the Prince of Darkness" (p. 164). This ascent of his goddess from the diabolic leaves Cusins able to embrace the Undershaft creed with the incidental hope of working its improvement; initially, he can prove his right to inherit the firm by means of "subterfuge" and "casuistry" (p. 165). In other words, the devious application of his intelligence is one of the several lessons Cusins has just learned, and he has learned it under the joint influences of Undershaft and his daughter.

The element of "ethical discussion" in the play now begins to intensify. Undershaft gives forth his "Armourer's Faith", the gist of which concerns the free access of mankind to the means of combat. But though Cusins objects to Undershaft's "morality", saying that he is not going to put his neck into *its* noose when he has just finished extricating that neck from his own, he at once confesses that he is not in search of power—though he

has more power than Undershaft himself (pp. 168-69).
But Cusins defines power as "will"; to which Undershaft
"enigmatically" admits that the place is driven by "A will
of which I am a part" (p. 169). Cusins accurately describes
this sort of talk as "metaphysics" in advising Barbara not
to listen, for she regards what Undershaft has said as
"laying a snare for my soul". And though the latter freely
admits that he lacks the power to "make courage and
conviction", he does most earnestly seek to "hypnotize"
Barbara—who now admits that such power, to be
effective, must come from without: must take over the
individual and possess him (pp. 169-70).

But now the play turns to the rout of conventional
Crosstianity. Barbara admits that what she had thought
was the "power of God" working through her has proved
to be a "rock" that has collapsed in an earthquake, and
was not "eternal" at all (p. 170). Barbara's Salvation
Army Christianity—or any form of the Christianity that
Christ described as a "rock"—is not worth holding on to;
Undershaft advises, "Scrap it" (p. 170). And now
Undershaft—or Shaw—is in full cry, reciting the "seven
deadly sins" that result from "the crime of poverty";
nothing will change until force, the willingness to kill, is
added to conviction—and Cusins is forced to agree that
Undershaft is right, though he wishes it were otherwise
(pp. 171-75). But Undershaft is not through yet: he rages
at Cusins' dependence on "Ought!" (p. 175). What is
needed, according to the play at this point, is a man ready
to live in the world as it is, and not one guided by mere
metaphysics.

With her young flock rushing to agree with Undershaft,
Lady Brit lapses into silence, but not before calling
everyone a name in order to clear her "conscience";
among these are the terms "Jesuit" for Cusins and
"lunatic" for Barbara (p. 176). I take the application of
these terms to be more than casual; they define the
means by which Lady Brit's conventional Crosstianity
has been defeated. Cusins has, for once, applied his
intellectual power to a situation which requires force and
effort; Barbara has allowed herself to be carried away by

an exterior will. Shaw has, like several other playwrights, used sexual identifications to represent dualities in human responses to given situations. Logos is about to be wedded to Life-Force, and will to power.

Now begins a recital of diversions to be avoided: good conscience and its claims; pity, love (the point is blunted by the obvious case before us), and forgiveness (pp. 177-78). Acting as though one false move will cost him Barbara, Cusins finally accepts the position as Undershaft's assistant and heir (p. 180). That he is selling his soul in the bargain does not upset him, for at least this time he is doing it "for reality and for power" (pp. 180-81). It is "power for the world" he wants, while Barbara insists on "spiritual power" (p. 181); but Cusins answers that all power is spiritual, "higher", as soon as it is devoted to giving common men the means of destroying their enemies, thereby making "war on war" (p. 182). Dreading her answer, he asks Barbara if their relationship has now ended. But her immediate reassurance restores Cusins' jubilation: he mimes a flourish of Salvation Army drumsticks (p. 182).

Barbara's actions at this point are curious, and occupy audience attention until the end of the play. At Cusins' display of joy, she flashes him an angry look; if only, she cries, she could "get away from you and from father and from it all" and "fly away to heaven". Yet she cannot, as she confesses; there is no turning one's back on life, especially its wicked side: "life is all one" (pp. 182-83). Barbara renounces the class into which she was born, for she comes "straight out of the heart of the whole people" (p. 183). With this extraordinary utterance, Barbara not only precludes settling into bourgeois comfort with her Dolly, but also lays claim to being a kind of representative being, force, or agency. She will be the spirit of the people, the popular spirit—immense, epic, and divine as a figure out of Delacroix. She embraces life and its struggles; she is to be the Life-Force, rarified by commitment to justice.

What happens next is so rare a dramatic moment that its full implications are seldom realized in the theatre. For though Shaw finds it necessary to anchor his heroine to earth with guy-ropes of humour, what happens is patent enough in his own stage-direction: "She is transfigured" (p. 184). The lines accompanying this transformation are just as striking:

> BARBARA: . . . I have got rid of the bribe of bread. I have got rid of the bribe of heaven. Let God's work be done for its own sake: the work he had to create us to do because it cannot be done except by living men and women. When I die, let him be in my debt, not I in his; and let me forgive him as becomes a woman of my rank.
>
> CUSINS: Then the way of life lies through the factory of death?
>
> BARBARA: Yes, through the raising of hell to heaven and of man to God, through the unveiling of an eternal light in the Valley of the Shadow. [*Seizing him with both hands*] Oh, did you think my courage would never come back? did you believe that I was a deserter? that I, who have stood in the streets, and taken my people to my heart, and talked of the holiest and greatest things with them, could ever turn back and chatter foolishly to fashionable people about nothing in a drawing room? Never, never, never, never: Major Barbara will die with the colours. Oh! and I have my dear little Dolly boy still; and he has found me my place and my work. Glory Hallelujah! [*She kisses him*].
>
> (p. 184)

The play ends in laughter, as I have noted: both Sarah (imitating a bicycle horn to get her mother to move) and Barbara (tugging at her mother's skirts) seem to Lady Brit to have turned into children again, incapable of independent action. But what Barbara wants is Lady Brit's help selecting "a house in the village to live in with Dolly"; things have changed forever in a way Barbara's mother will never comprehend (pp. 184-85).

Undershaft, presumably, does. Cusins has told him that Barbara "has gone right up into the skies" (pp. 184-85), a telling pun to make in a munitions works. Barbara is indeed "blown up", arisen, exultant; she is beside herself (ecstatic). How else could she describe her conversations with the "people" as being of the "holiest and greatest things" or speak of a "rank" from which she might grant God forgiveness? She is the Spirit of the people itself, and now she has taken a husband who is intellectual power itself: that is, will. The devil has done

43

his work again; Lucifer has borne in Light. As in the Biblical accounts of Christ's transfiguration, a euphoric Barbara has been borne up in a vision of Light; both her appearance and her significance have been altered. What Cusins' Plato knew of as transcendental nobility, truth, and beauty, is embodied in Barbara. She is free at last. The apostles who accompanied Jesus wished to erect tents or tabernacles, but Barbara's monument is already there, in Undershaft's pleasant hell: "a house in the village". And she is there, like Christ, to raise the lower to the higher, and do for mankind what only the divine in man can do.

In the account of Dives and Lazarus, and in the narrative of the Transfiguration, there is a merging of values which will be referred to elsewhere in this volume. The prophets Moses and Elias unite the two events, both accompanying Jesus in his moment of ecstasy, and also serving as the voices which a selfish mankind has refused to heed. The latter condition has brought about the necessity of a redemptive act, a death of Christ. In Shaw's view, the question may be asked differently: will mankind find in itself the power to make changes for the better, and thus acknowledge the rule of the Life-Force, the Barbara within? *Major Barbara* provides a model; it does not answer the question.

In the dramatic structure of this play, so peculiar in its echoes of Greek antecedents, Undershaft comes equipped as *deus-cum-machina*, yet nearly disappears from view before the conclusion—the values of which are provided, in what is recognizably the modern manner, by the other characters themselves. But nearly a decade later, Ezra Pound gave a more famous—and less optimistic—expression to many of these same themes in "Hugh Selwyn Mauberley":

> The tea-rose tea-gown, etc.
> Supplants the mousseline of Cos,
> The pianola "replaces"
> Sappho's barbitos.
>
> Christ follows Dionysus,
> Phallic and ambrosial
> Made way for macerations;
> Caliban casts out Ariel.

All things are a flowing,
Sage Heracleitus says;
But a tawdry cheapness
Shall outlast our days.

Even the Christian beauty
Defects—after Samothrace;
We see *Tò kalón*
Decreed in the market place.

All men, in law, are equals.
Free of Pisistratus,
We choose a knave or an eunuch
To rule over us.

O bright Apollo,
tín ándra, tín héroa, tín theòn,
What god, man, or hero
Shall I place a tin wreath upon![4]

The question persists. But Shaw's version—perhaps because the merger of Christ and Dionysus constitutes a kind of historical imperative—is the more optimistic one.

NOTES

1 George Bernard Shaw, *Major Barbara*, in *Collected Plays with Their Prefaces: 3* (New York, 1975). All page references appear parenthetically within my text.
2 The New Testament references are to Matthew 17:1-13, Mark 9:2-13, Luke 9:28-36, and II Peter 1:16-18.
3 Euripides, *The Bacchae*, trans. William Arrowsmith, in *Euripides III*, ed. David Grene and Richard Lattimore (New York, 1959), pp. 397-98.
4 Ezra Pound, *Personae* (New York, 1926), p. 189.

4

Synge's Savage Sermon: *The Playboy of The Western World*

What the Greeks would have turned into tragedy—some did—becomes tragi-comedy at the hands of John Millington Synge. The oedipal conflict that lies at the core of *The Playboy of the Western World* (1907)[1] animates more than a critique of Irish social values as parodied by the community he depicts, a hamlet off in the supposedly more authentically Irish West. The play's final spectacle is a profound revolt against the traditional values and norms; with it accomplished, "the West's awake" indeed. Christy Mahon's declaration of independence is meant as a model for Ireland generally, its value underscored by Pegeen Mike's last wail of loss:

> PEGEEN: . . . *(Putting her shawl over her head and breaking out into wild lamentations.)* Oh my grief, I've lost him surely. I've lost the only Playboy of the Western World.
>
> (p. 80)

Pegeen has lost her Playboy because she did not trust her heart at the crucial moment of decision in the play; in denying Christy just when he had become assured of attaining real manhood, she missed the opportunity to profit by what, implicitly, has become Christy's gospel to the people of Mayo. For Christy is arguably a parodic Christ, or at least a Christ-bearer—as his name suggests. Synge employs him to point up "the villainy of Mayo" (p. 80) and, by extension, the shortcomings of those Irish values which are ironically tied in theory to the name of Christ.

Through the manipulation of Christian references and values, Synge drives home his message about the need for change—not only in the hoary practices of land-division, but more importantly in sexual mores. Those mores can be called "Freudian" not in the aforementioned oedipal sense but in the broader, more pervasive sense of the repression of deep-seated feelings and longings, especially sexual ones. This chapter is not intended as an exercise in psychological terminology, however, but rather as an examination of *The Playboy of the Western World* as a dramatic plea for what are by now commonly-accepted behavioural norms and principles of action. It will therefore focus on the contrapuntal development of Pegeen Mike ("wild-looking but fine" as the stage-directions describe her [p. 7]) and her lost lover Christy Mahon—a character I would term the evangelist of the inner call of the passions. Through a consistent fabric of religious references, Synge subtly ties his social gospel to the presumed basis of local custom: the Christian Church and its explicit prescriptions for action.

The underlying themes of *The Playboy* are loneliness and sexual non-fulfilment, themes depicted through the absence of satisfying sexual communion of any sort. Widows and orphans abound, as well as death and sterile marriage, but nowhere do we glimpse the possibility of real sexual health. It is indeed "a queer lot these times to go troubling the Holy Father on his sacred seat" (p. 9), as Pegeen puts it; but that is because—discounting the naivety of her discussion with Shawn, with its presumption that the Pope is interested in what they are up to out there in the West of Ireland—mental and physical defectives have taken the place of the heroes of the recent past, men who were distinguished by their violent relationships with each other and with Nature (and in the process became attractive to the young women of the vicinity) (p. 9). Cleverly, Synge avoids placing onstage the cassocked Father Reilly, but the latter's opinions are enormously important in influencing the actions of the onstage characters. *Playboy* is a drama of missed connections—of what might have been—and its hidden priest is a major factor in what eventually occurs.

The dramatic contrast is between the offstage voice of established Truth, therefore, and the existential quest which actualized in the person of Christy Mahon. Synge uses the stock dramatic device "the arrival of the stranger" to create the mix of forces out of which a set of new values will emerge. When we first hear of Christy's arrival, it is through the revelations of Shawn and, later, Michael that they have heard "groaning" in the ditch outside (pp. 10, 12); yet neither of these presumed Christians has responded to the sound of a fellow-human in need. "For the love of God", Shawn begs Pegeen, let him not be revealed as knowing anything of the desperate stranger (p. 10). Having failed this Good-Samaritan test, Shawn and Michael must deal with the plight of Pegeen, who has called herself "lonesome" but has been consigned—Michael says—to Shawn's care by "the will of God" (pp. 8, 11). But Shawn begs the saints to help him avoid being left alone with Pegeen (p. 12); here and throughout the play, religious references—though they abound—are nearly always in effect made ironically, for their contexts are nearly always the opposite of credible application's coverage. In general, they create a tonality of repressiveness, the sort which Michael underscores when he holds up the coat of the frightened-away Shawn, saying, "Well, there's the coat of a Christian man" (p. 13), quite without apparent critical intent. A Christian man, by this implicit definition, is one without sexual integrity, a sexual cipher—no danger to anyone's morals, and not much fun, either. Shawn goes home "lonesome" (p. 14), much like everyone else.

But this is a society with its values reversed: when Christy enters with the customary invocations of God's blessings (p. 14), it is with the assurance that even though he is the son of a late "strong farmer", he has done nothing which is not "decent": i.e., nothing of a sexual nature (p. 15). "With the help of God" he has killed his father, though, and may "the Holy Immaculate Mother . . . intercede for his soul" (p. 17). The place of the deed is as remote—thanks to Christy's suspiciousness—as Oedipus's crossroads; but Christy is suddenly valuable for the spirit he has demostrated at long range, for—as Jimmy says—"Bravery's a treasure in a lonesome place", and a lad like Christy might face the devil (p. 19). "Well, glory be to God!" is Christy's reaction, so abruptly does he realize what a commodity his storied violence has become (p. 19). With a frank expression of incipient lust, Pegeen sends Shawn off to "the holy brotherhoods, and leave that lad to me" (p. 21). Nothing like Christy has come to town before, thanks to the Church's dire controls.

Without meaning to play games with names, I must draw attention to Synge's evident emphasis on those in *Playboy*. Christy Mahon's, whether or not one accepts the notion of an implicit Christ-referent contained within it, is surely the epitome of a sort of ordinariness—so much so, that one is surprised to hear Pegeen praise his "quality name" (p. 22). What can she possibly mean, if some impossibly erudite and distinctly Irish association is not meant to be conveyed? For what could be commoner, on the face of things, than "Christy Mahon", Christian Man, the Irish Everyman? Surely he does not possess anything like a "quality name" in the usual sense; I would myself relate this name-play to what is said of Old Mahon two pages later, when Christy refers to the "sons and daughters walking all great states and territories of the world" he has (p. 25)—the implication being that Old Mahon is somehow meant to be taken as Father Ireland, with numerous children scattered over the other continents of the earth, with Christy being the younger version of the same native stock. These Mahons appear as ordinary as Chekhov's cherry orchard, itself the image for great Mother Russia. In other words, though they appear to be by definition unexceptional, they are as well-designedly symbolic, in this case of the Irish male's dilemma.

It is Pegeen who makes the association between Christy's newfound passion and the craft of poetry:

> PEGEEN: . . . I've heard all times it's the poets are your like, fine fiery fellows with great rages when their temper's roused.
>
> (p. 23)

And Christy accepts this characterization of himself when he admits that the leisurely admiration of nature has been his chief means of subsistence thus far, whereas his father has taken a cruder—even aboriginal—route, "going out into the yard as naked as an ash tree in the moon of May, and shying clods against the visage of the stars . . ." (p. 25). Between the father and the son has been the difference between a manic stasis and the urge to rebel, between a classic sort of raw defiance and the need to turn defiance into action, even the act of flight. Star imagery pervades the play, and chucking clods skyward its means of expressing resentment.

It is a poet's resentment, and a poet's expression, however heavy-handed the means of bringing the expression forth may be. Both Christy and Pegeen are partial "orphans", and by extension the Widow Quin is similarly dispossessed of kindred (pp. 27-8). An act of indirection has caused the death of her man—by blood poisoning—which enables her to join the others as receptive agencies awaiting fulfilment—for as the Widow says, "There's great temptation in a man did slay his da" (p. 28), and Christy ought therefore to forsake the company of Pegeen. Is the Widow a witch, or merely a conspirer (p. 29)? Whatever the truth about *her*, Synge ends his Act with Christy's descent into comfort, and with his wish he had killed his father earlier (had he only known the rewards awaiting the deed) (p. 30). Again, religion's presence in the play serves to subvert its ostensible value system, and the verbal traces of its existence mock its influence.

Considering *Playboy*'s reputation as the play that provoked riots by mentioning "shifts" (p. 75), it is astonishing to realize the extent of serious damage Synge did the existent Irish system *without* calling attention to the fact, without provoking demonstrations of outrage of any sort. The sexuality pervading the opening of Act II is a case in point. We move from the narcissistic act of examining his new image in the mirror glass (p. 31); plainly, his new sexual appeal is the result of his desperado's reputation. And when the four girls from the neighbourhood come in, the verbal concretions are stunningly earthy, an innuendo of Mae-Western proportions. As Sara puts on Christy's boots, the talk is sensual—all of the senses are involved—and their adoption of Christy's air of sexual attractiveness is quite apparent (pp. 32-3). The girls present the young man with gifts of sensual value, and the emphasis is on his sampling the quality of what they have brought. "Hold out your hand and you'll see it's no lie I'm telling you", says Sara, handing Christy duck eggs (p. 33), and Susan brings butter, Honour cake, and Nelly an especially blessed chicken:

> NELLY: And I brought you a little laying pullet—boiled and all she is—was crushed at the fall of night by the curate's car.

Feel the fat of that breast, mister.
CHRISTY: It's bursting, surely.

(p. 34)

Nelly's throaty exchange with Christy is immediately followed by Sara's mocking merger of the elements of this scene: sensuality, narcissism, and religion. Why won't Christy touch the pullet, she asks; is his "right hand too sacred for to use at all?" No, it is because he is holding a looking glass behind his back: "Them that kills their fathers is a vain lot surely" (p. 34). Only the Widow's interruption ends this interplay, and that is on the new note of game-playing, the sporting contests to which Christy must now address himself—in order to become a true "playboy", a defeater of the world.

Prodded by the Widow Quin, Christy admits that it was not in fact land-lust at all, but fear of marriage to his former nurse, that drove him to parricidal violence (pp. 35-6); the specifics of the murder attempt, which may indeed be pure products of Christy's imagination and therefore highly questionable, involve elaborate geographical referents (a habit of the play's characters) that add up to a cross upon the ground (p. 37), but also establish clear parallels to the violent career of the Widow Quin (p. 37). It is Sara who recognizes the connection, and makes the couple join arms while she proposes a toast to "the wonders of the western world", all of whom seem to be frauds and lawbreakers of various sorts. Quite plainly, the society of this "western world", long suffering its English occupation, has had its values overturned: what undermines the system deserves the admiration of all.

Pegeen's re-entry shifts the focus of the scene. The "new" Christy tries to regain mastery of the situation by retelling his story (pp. 38-9), but Pegeen counters by filling his mind with an horrific account of the hanging that awaits his murdering son:

PEGEEN: . . . it'd make the green stones cry itself to think of you swaying and swiggling at the butt of a rope, and you with a fine, stout neck, God bless you! the way you'd be a half an hour, in great anguish, getting your death.

(p. 40)

Christy replies by projecting himself as an Old Testament wanderer, rather unlearnedly (p. 40); the discussion turns to

51

the topic of loneliness, which Pegeen has already confessed to sharing. Christy's needs are stated drastically: he turns to "women and girls the way the needy fallen spirits do be looking on the Lord" (p. 40); by revealing that his loneliness is that of "the moon of dawn", he regains his place in Pegeen's heart (p. 42). Admiring the "savagery" that enabled Christy to slay his da, Pegeen creates an implied equation between loneliness and savagery (passion), its answer and its ease (p. 42). For a woman must admire "a lad" with "a mighty spirit in him and a gamey heart" (p. 43). The spiritual equivalence of passion and isolation have been established; now the question becomes one of whether or not Pegeen will understand in time.

Shawn's re-entry introduces the financial element thus far lacking in the play. Trying to bribe Christy (p. 44), he reminds us again of the economic motivation Synge sees providing a distinctive cant to Irish domestic relations. The clothes that Shawn can afford become, when Christy puts them on, the basis of a new personality: Christy is thus prepared to play the "playboy" in the games, as well as—in the irony of the play's title—to play the man in real life. As the Widow Quin tells Shawn, "It's true all girls are fond of courage and do hate the like of you" (p. 45); it is Christy and not Shawn who is capable, ultimately, of living up to the implications of the clothes (i.e., the role) he dons. Filling clothes, filling roles, becomes the existential heart of Christy's "message"—the gospel he preaches by example. Though at this stage of things he is more swagger than genuine man (witness his heaven-beseeching double-take upon his father's arrival two pages later; p. 47), Christy is already on his way. He will first have to prove not only his aggressive capacity at self-projection, but his honestly romantic aptitude as well.

Old Mahon's appearance (his very name is a pun on his essential significance) confirms what we have suspected about Christy the pseudo-playboy: he was always the dreamer; he was vain; he loved nature; and he was afraid of girls. As of yet he has not learned to love, and is therefore without the capacity for poetic articulation to which his nature tends; he is thus capable of taking only a child's first tentative but necessarily violent steps towards self-definition—a blow of which his father seems distinctly proud (pp. 48-9). Yet though Christy's bravado has faded with his father's rising from the dead (p. 50), the chief element in his fear seems to be the new one of what Pegeen will think of him now—not to mention the other "fine women of Ireland". Because he has seen "the love-light of the star of knowledge shining from [Pegeen's] brow" (p. 51), Christy's life has been changed: acknowledging their interdependence has given him the ability to make "poetry talk", as the Widow Quin mocks his speech and its subject; though the Widow presents herself to him in descriptive terms that emphasize their similarities, it is Pegeen that Christy longs for—because she has restored him to heaven's favour (p. 52). And thus it is not surprising to find Act II concluding with Christy begging the Widow to help him win back Pegeen, promising her that he will "be asking God to stretch a hand to [her] in the hour of death, and lead [her] short cuts through the Meadows of Ease, and up the floor of Heaven to the Footstool of the Virgin's Son" (p. 53). As the Widow admits, "There's praying", and Christy's subsequent plea that she help and "save" him "for the love of Christ" is by this time no accident, for Pegeen has given him a glimpse of salvation; thanks to the redemptive power of love, Christy Mahon has been able to approach not only poetic utterance but something of genuine piety—in marked contrast to the play's generally ironic misuse of religious references.

In Act III, Christy's new personality develops further, distancing him rapidly from the other characters who, unlike himself, learn nothing during the course of the play. Thus we find him performing prodigies of all sorts at the local festival— Christy's "miracles", if you wish—and in the process emphasizing his own growing isolation (pp. 54-5). Jimmy and Philly react to Mahon's skull-wound with an apposite "Glory be to God!" and speculation on the wonders of the human heart; interestingly, the full range of such wonders, according to *Playboy*, appears to encompass only the vagaries of violence and romance (p. 56). The pairing of love and violence is an acute bit of psychological foresight on Synge's part, a dramatic statement oddly predictive of Jerry's gospel in Albee's *Zoo Story*. The alternative to the love/violence initiation would appear to be a deadening of the spirit, the sort of loneliness which now Old Mahon complains of (p. 58), joining his voice to what seems to be a general chorus of local feeling (or its lack). Small wonder

Old Mahon cannot reconcile the winner of the mule-race with the son he remembers, for Christy has changed in the interim, enough for "logic" to make the old man disbelieve the evidence of his own senses (pp. 59-60).

Old Mahon has reached a peak of excitement during the running of the distant mule-race with a burst of spontaneous poetry: "Look at the mule he has, kicking the stars." And indeed we might expect star-kicking to be a natural image to this man who has expressed his own resentment at life—in his son's telling of it—by shying clods at the stars. This son he does not recognize has done what he himself could not; so that when Old Mahon thinks he recognizes Christy after all, he shouts "It's Christy! by the stars of God!" (p. 60). The others turn his accusations of madness against him, so that Old Mahon begins to accept their name for his mental state; pathetically, he admits, denies, doubts, and then accepts the view that he is indeed mad: "It's true mankind is the divil when your head's astray" (pp 61-2). Synge thus has introduced the notion that the individual with an idea contrary to society's will be termed mad by that society, and soon it will be Christy's turn to be described as crazy for his singular opinions (esp. p. 74). In *The Playboy of the Western World*, then, we are shown a social context in which the attainment of selfhood is tantamount to accepting public scorn for one's "mad" pursuits.

Christy's awards for his athletic and other attainments are appropriate to his newfound image: a bagpipes, a poet's fiddle, and a blackthorn (p. 63); they are the trappings of the lover he has become. And they equip him for the scene which follows: abruptly left alone, he and Pegeen exchange their feelings in one of the loveliest love scenes ever written (pp. 64-6); in it, young Christy reaches after the fantastic conceit that sums up all he has become, the formerly lonesome man with his formerly lonesome beloved: ". . . I'd feel a kind of pity for the Lord God is all ages sitting lonesome in his golden chair" (p. 64). And they would spend Good Friday wandering as lovers in the fields! Indeed, each lover states that, in effect, he/she has found a heaven in the other one. Unremarkable singly, these usages create a telling pattern throughout the play, one in which— without, I hope, forcing such parallels as exist—Synge can be seen to have created Christy, Christ and Christ-bearer, as a bringer of good news—a carrier of the ideas of love as the key to human development back to a community founded on principles supposedly Christian, presumably the religion of love.

So that though—after the completion of the love scene, with Christy and Pegeen agreed that love has made them epic in stature, in effect (p.66)—Michael returns in time to compare Old Mahon to "holy Joseph in the days gone by", I would not leap to take this reference as confirmation of Christy's symbolic status; Synge does not work that way, and the Joseph involved is likelier the Old Testament figure sold by his brothers into bondage (p. 67). Synge's way is rather to contrast the way of Mahon with the habits of Mayo, as when Michael refers without apparent irony to Shawn as "that shy and decent Christian I have chosen for my daughter's hand" (p. 67). Nothing has changed in Mayo—except in the mind of Pegeen, who has learned at least that Christy bears the marks of manhood that Shawn surely lacks; though she herself is without sufficient insight or courage to break with her own environment and its intellectual limitations, she is wise enough to observe of Shawn, specifying his lacks, that he has "no savagery or fine words in him at all" (p. 68). Savagery and fine words are indeed an interesting, even unusual, combination; yet Synge pairs the two as though they were the marks of manhood, the gifts of self-attainment. In Christy, of course, they result from love, which itself is the reciprocity of comforting mutual images between himself and Pegeen Mike.

When Pegeen speaks out on Christy's behalf, it is in defiance of her own father's wishes, for he has an eye to Shawn's property; yet her determination, together with Christy's confidence ("I'm mounted on the springtide of the stars of luck"), apparently carry the day (p. 70). And Michael can always console himself with the progeny this "daring" fellow will likely engender (p. 71). It is a moment of Old Testament solemnity, almost, this blessing of their union; yet the play turns Biblically heavy almost at once, as the returning Mahon enters (Pegeen wonders if he has risen from the dead), beats Christy, and in turn is denied by his son (p. 71). "Rise up now to retribution, and come on with me", Old Mahon orders Christy; and Pegeen turns against her man, thinking she has fallen in love with a figure of deceit alone (p. 72). It is not the blow Christy gave him that Old Mahon resents, but the former self he thinks his son still owns: "the sins of the whole world are committed" by such feckless types, he thinks. Christy calls upon "the name of the Almighty God" (p. 73), but Old Mahon bids him be still; the isolation of the son is complete, for Pegeen will not have him now.

Ironically enough, it is Pegeen's intelligence (or, more aptly, the way his love for her has set his own intelligence in motion) that Christy adores: "But what did I want crawling forward to scorch my understanding at her flaming brow?" (p. 73). She is his Eve, but also his Tree of Knowledge. The crowd sets Mahon against Mahon, with the result that the two of them defy their tormentors together, then run outdoors for a final showdown; Christy's offstage violence, though real enough for the villagers to witness it, is meant to win Pegeen back. An extraordinary juxtaposition of effects follows the Widow Quin's urging that Christy forsake Pegeen:

> CHRISTY: It's Pegeen I'm seeking only, and what'd I care if you brought me a drift of chosen females, standing in their shifts itself, maybe, from this place to the Eastern World?
> SARA (*runs in, pulling off one of her petticoats*): They're going to hang him. (*Holding out petticoat and shawl.*) Fit these upon him, and let him run off to the east.
>
> (p. 75)

Had the original audience that was so bothered by the word "shifts" stayed quiet and attentive, they would have noted the even more shocking quality of Sara's gesture. Urging Christy to flee in the garments of a woman is advice that might have been taken by a Shawn, but to Christy it is a symbolic emasculation he wants no part of. A visual metaphor of certain power, this petticoat-fastening forces the audience to consider what is happening to Christy, whatever it thinks of him as a character. These are clothes, at any rate, which imply a role Christy has no intention of adopting.

However, Christy is mistaken in Pegeen; she is horrified by his violent deed, and takes the lead in capturing her lover for the authorities to hang. Though her statement of belief has been considered the arguable "moral" of the play—

PEGEEN: I'll say, a strange man is a marvel, with his mighty talk; but what's a squabble in your back-yard, and the blow of a loy, have taught me that there's a great gap between a gallous story and a dirty deed.   (p. 77)

—it hides the fact that Pegeen has become Christy's Judas, making his capture and execution on the gallows-tree a real possibility. Thus the lover's act is not a union, but a betrayal. (And we might note that Christy's act was no wilful murder, but instead the frenzied act of a desperate man and, for all of that, non-fatal for the second time.) What with the biting and the burning and the crawling around on all fours that take place in the next few moments of the play, not to mention the shouting and the hurling of oaths and threats, we are entitled to think that Synge has given us Mayo County's bogman act as the play's crisis, but in fact this reversion to general primitivism is only the counterpoint to Christy's full emergence as a man (pp. 78-9). It is ironic that Pegeen first denies, then threatens to "scorch" (and indeed finally does burn) the body of her lover, the man who wanted to "scorch" his understanding "at her flaming brow". More important, though, is Christy's full embrace of manhood, his joyous decision to go down fighting his enemies, to accept the consequences of his deeds, and to go to hell if needs be.

Irony, indeed. "O, glory be to God!" screams Christy as he receives his punishing burn, at which his twice-resurrected father crawls in. The two men stand together against "the villainy of Mayo", and Old Mahon praises God in words which echo his son's recent cry of pain, but are meant to welcome back his blessed craziness with a smile (p. 80). It is this ending that we began with, and I would emphasize the cleavage here between the keening Pegeen, to whom "normal" life has been restored, and the positive gaiety with which the Mahons make their way down the road out of town. "Ten thousand blessings" are Christy's parting grant, for now he'll go "romancing" until "the dawning of the judgment day" (p. 80). He is a free man indeed—freed of convention, respectability, and the strictures of a misinterpreted religion—and has no more need to shy clods at the stars than his father does. He is not "crazy", though, as the old man says *he* is; he is simply a lover and a poet now. A man, redeemed, having suffered for sins, having raised the dead (himself included), but having escaped the fatal Tree. Pegeen has truly lost the "only" Playboy, the social revolutionary who refuses to base his independence on his father's death, or sell his heart. He has overturned the moneychangers' tables. Synge was telling Ireland to go and do likewise.

NOTE

1   *The Complete Works of John M. Synge* (New York, 1936). All page references appear parenthetically within my text.

5

Brecht's Judging Jesus: *The Caucasian Chalk Circle*

That Bertolt Brecht often wrote about situations or on themes that are religious in nature or connection (*Saint Joan of the Stockyards, Galileo*) is evident enough; but that he also employed *echt*-Christian sacrificial gestures in crucial dramatic moments (*Mother Courage, The Good Woman of Setzuan*) has surely been less often considered. Though certain of his plays have been called "parables for the theatre", moreover, there seems to have been no great attention given to the extent to which *The Caucasian Chalk Circle*[1] is ultimately not unlike a tale told by, and about, a kind of secular Christ—the temporary judge, Azdak. Nor is it surprising that Azdak is presented as an instructional *improvement* on the original, given Brecht's leftist didacticism, and given the sentimentality that Marxism sets out to accomplish what Christianity has been content only to preach. And ultimately, the pragmatic socialism of the division of the land to make the greatest good for the greatest number possible is not so far from Christ's division of the loaves and fishes, nor indeed from the distribution of Communion. Indeed, the text supports the latter interpretation, for by breaking "statute and rule" "like a loaf" to feed "the folk", Azdak creates the example of a "miraculous" redistribution of resources (p. 570) that presumably informs the watching onstage audience of Caucasian peasants, wondering what use to make of their liberated piece of land, how to go and do likewise.

It is entirely possible—though I find the possibility more than a bit chilling—that the "great judge" the play wishes to

59

honour was the twentieth century's ultimate Caucasian, Josef Stalin; otherwise, one is hard put to explain the choice of setting for this dramatization of what is called a Chinese folk-tale (except as one of many locales affording plots of suitably "liberated" land in the wake of World War II). Be that as it may, Azdak is shown, like a Molière king, to be the answer to his people's prayers for justice, and in the process he reconciles the dilemma of power and caring which, in *The Good Woman of Setzuan*, causes a cleavage of character without simultaneously providing an "answer". In *CCC*, that dichotomy is part of the play's structure; for outside of the tedious (to anyone but a committed socialist-realist) framing materials, the play consists of five acts, but one of the central characters does not make his first appearance until the fourth of them. It is as though the helpless goodness of *Good Woman* were *CCC*'s given problem, and as though the personification of benign state power in Azdak were the answer the earlier play had lacked. In theoretical Marxist terms, Azdak is the synthesis the play demands—a revolutionary synthesis, of course, who exists *only* within revolutionary times, unstable by definition.

In the three acts preceding Azdak's entrance, we are shown a world devoid of charity. The conspicuous exceptions are Grusha's adoptive affection for Michael, and the soldier Simon's tender feeling for Grusha. Pure love, both of the parent-child variety and that between man and woman, is shown to be incapable of sustaining itself in the hostile environment of the play, which is itself a reflection of the real world we inhabit. These love-relationships, so touchingly presented, are like the Christian Gospel in terms of lack of supportive power, and Brecht intends to show us the political remedy he thinks not only desirable but necessary. For during the first three acts, Grusha encounters the various mechanisms of the unfeeling system, the status quo: the state, the military, and the bourgeois society (the capitalist ethic combined with institutional religion). Only Azdak can cut the knot that threatens to strangle Love in its embrace.

The opening scene of the first act, we must remember, is devoted to a coup that changes nothing for the common folk; by setting this event during the Christian Eastertide, Brecht employs conventional Christianity to underscore the irony of radical change that makes no real difference: the season of hope means only a brutal chaos without an intelligence to control the power unleashed (as happens in Shaw's *Major Barbara*). In this Easter scene, Brecht plays the menace of the coming revolt against the bland pomposity and selfishness of the Governor and his wife, who ignore the clear warnings of danger in order to proceed with an Easter celebration that is without real religious meaning and merely the occasion for their own egoistic indulgence. Though it is Easter, Grusha must work—procuring a goose for the Governor's banquet. "But the goose was not eaten this time . . ." (pp. 508-10), for as the Story Teller taunts the captured Governor,

> Between the Easter mass and the Easter meal
> You are walking to the place whence no one returns.
>
> (p. 512)

This is an Easter, then, that has no Resurrection.

Yet even in the midst of turmoil, the possibility of a redemptive gesture is set in motion by the telescoped courtship of Grusha and Simon. Their touching exchange, their agreement to wed pledged with Simon's gift of a silver cross that had been his mother's (p. 515), is sanctified, as it were, by Grusha's succumbing to the "terrible . . . seductive power of goodness" (p. 521) when she picks up the abandoned, supposedly precious, child of the Governor and his wife. In other words, the child of their love appears to its eventual mother almost at once, as if by the fiat of a Holy Spirit. And though I wish to argue that Azdak plays the role of secular Christ in *CCC*, I must acknowledge that the infant Michael is himself possessed of redemptive qualities, and transforms the Grusha personage into a sort of Blessed Virgin. Almost at once, Grusha and Michael are forced into a "Flight into the Northern Mountains", where one soldier ironically berates another as "a hollow reed and a tinkling cymbal"—not, as in the Bible, for lack of love, but for inadequacy of sadistic cruelty (p. 524). Indeed, Grusha's adoption of Michael is the beginning of a "miracle" of a kind, because in Brecht's improvement of the Chinese story-source (or of the Biblical story of Solomon's judgement), Grusha is finally acknowledged to be the child's "true" mother—the one, that is, who deserves to be the agent of

61

his upbringing. It is as though the "speaking" infant had made his own Annunciation.

For Michael has serious work to do, a role that is near-Messianic to play: a Father's business to attend to. As Grusha sings in the act-ending "Song of the Child",

> Your father is a thief,
> Your mother is a whore,
> And all good people
> Will kneel at your door.
>
> The sons of the tiger
> Are the horse's brothers,
> The child of the snake
> Brings milk to the mothers.

(p. 534)

Like that Caucasian field in dispute, like the property of an entrenched capitalist class or the children of that class, the products of the corrupt system can be refreshed and redeemed for the use of the new society. Michael is the Saviour who needs saving first, and Grusha is the Blessed Mother who will make both savings possible by her action and her example.

Therefore the archetypal simplicity of Grusha's trek northward can be credited to its awakening of vestigial religious consciousness—or myth-awareness—in its Western audience, with its echoes of Bethlehem, and the Flight into Egypt. More striking still is the darkly comic parody of Madonna-and-Child paintings Grusha provides when, unable to afford milk for Michael, she gives him her empty breast to suck at: "There's nothing there, but you *think* you're drinking, and that's something" (p. 523). By combining the bleakly humorous with the truly pathetic here, Brecht not only allows Grusha to dramatize her folk-shrewdness in a telling way, but also underscores the mythic function of her role.

Yet Grusha does in the end buy the milk, and though she complains incessantly about the burden the child constitutes for her, she *acts* as incessantly on its behalf. Her behaviour is in obvious contrast with that of the "Christians" around her, who complain of the irreligious quality of her heroic crossing of the Rotten Bridge (p. 533), or who—like her "religious" sister-in-law (pp. 535-40)—worry more about scandal and a full belly than about a present case of real need. Of course, Brecht balances these examples with that of the good Peasant Woman, who takes in the temporarily "abandoned" Michael without ado (in fact refusing to think of taking him to the village priest) and without false piety (p. 526). Of course, she is also quick to save herself when the soldiers arrive; Brecht does not sentimentalize about poverty, finding it the corrupt effect of a corrupt cause. Instead, he argues for the bringing about of substantial change through the union of power and caring.

Grusha understands the necessity for this joining, as well as what its results would be. She picks up Michael naturally, "as the pear tree comes to the sparrows. And because a Christian bends down and picks up a crust of bread so nothing will go to waste" (p. 540). Hers is a distinctly socialist Christianity; and there is no place in the Grusinian scheme of things for her kind of goodness.

By way of active contrast, witness the drunken Monk who officiates at her forced wedding to the "dying" draft evader (a marriage which to Grusha insures Michael's safety, but to the people closely involved means the avoidance of scandal—for a price). This Monk works at bargain rates and even tries to sell the groom a bit of extreme unction. He is an improbable figure, hiding an endless supply of bottles beneath his soutane and praying in Latin (in the Caucasus of the Eastern Church). But he is more than simply the amiable boozer one often sees onstage; I suggest that he is Brecht's representative of an ineffectual institutional Christianity. His basic cynicism betrays itself on more than one occasion, as when the groom's mother finds him in the tavern mouthing a Brechtian motto: "The war is over, beware of the peace!" (p. 543). And in his easy, platitudinous resolution of the demands of this unusual wedding/funeral scene, his request for music that can serve as "either a subdued Wedding March or a spirited Funeral Dance", and his sly collusion with the uninvited musicians and the singing drunken peasant, one sees revealed a darkened spirit which uses alcohol as a refuge from the bitterness of frustration (pp. 543-44). We notice that only Azdak is, like this Monk, deeply "touched" by events in the play—and that in his case as well, the sentiment voiced is really the expression of a sarcasm (in Azdak's case, that the mention of estates is "proof of human feeling"; p. 580). The genuine piety of Grusha, when at the news of the war's end she kisses Simon's cross (p. 545), is unknown to general Grusinian experience. Azdak is what the drunken Monk should be, but cannot be.

Azdak enters the play at a moment of dramatic tension: the failure of the grown Michael to play the parts of either the Governor (his father) or his executioner adequately; the immediately subsequent, unhappy reunion of Grusha and Simon, the river of time flowing between them, and the scene concluding with the renunciation of the cross that had represented their mutual pledge; and the Ironshirts' capture of Michael and Grusha (pp. 548-52). Yet though the children's play, with its ironic (even chilling) dramatization of the theme of redemption, is juxtaposed in the fourth act (Part II, Section I) with Azdak's saving of the Grand Duke (the implications of these two scenes in turn providing the play's eventual resolution), Azdak's arrival is prepared for by nothing more than a piece of melodramatic rhetoric worthy of a soap-opera:

> Who will decide the case?
> To whom will the child be assigned?
> Who will the judge be? A good judge? A bad?
> The city was in flames.
> In the judge's seat sat Azdak.
>
> (p. 552)

Brecht's discarding of conventional dramatic rules of construction, returning as he does to the time of the initial scene in order to present a character totally unheard-of before, is as patent as it is deliberate; there is, however, a logic to his introduction of Azdak that goes beyond the capabilities of the classical syllogism. Azdak is the answer to the question the play asks; the opposition of apparently irreconcilable elements produces a political mutant, a synthesis of opposites. Of course, it is *because* "the city was in flames" that "in the judge's seat sat Azdak".

Azdak, a character born out of Marxist historical necessity, thus enters the play on a strong tide of inverted values and thwarted expectations. When the policeman Shauwa calls himself "just a Christian", Azdak goes him one better—he turns scholastic logic around to the defense of his own rabbit-poaching: "I'm a rabbit-eater, but you're a man-eater, Shauwa. And God will pass judgement on you. Shauwa, go home and repent" (p. 555). And immediately thereafter, he proves the point of his pragmatic "Christianity" by sheltering the Grand Duke, even showing the fugitive how to eat like a poor man. Of course, as one hopes Brecht himself saw, his play no more demands a Marxist solution than a strictly Christian one; his perception of needs and how to answer them is not much different from that of a nineteenth-century utilitarian, or a single-tax advocate like the American Henry George.

Yet like Christ, Azdak loves a paradox; he takes joy in explaining the "injustice" of the case of the Turkish landowner who was hanged in Tiflis for being a Turk—in spite of having been even more enthusiastically cruel to his peasants than his peers (p. 556). Immediately thereafter (in stage time), he denounces his sheltering of the Grand Duke to the Ironshirts (whom he thinks the agents of a real people's revolution) in a scene which could make satisfying sense only to a Stalinist. In "The Song of Injustice in Persia", Azdak sings of war's overturning of notions of worth (pp. 558-59), but once he sees his error in mistaking the Ironshirts for revolutionaries, he suffers the accusation that he came to "fish in the troubled waters" in silence (p. 559). The phrase may or may not remind one of Christ's image for apostolic labour, but the fact remains that Azdak does not act to seize power—in this case, the vacant judgeship—until confronted with the ugly opposition of the Fat Prince and his nephew. But with his linguistic cleverness, his attention to tricks of expression, Azdak easily disposes of the nephew's claim by trapping the young man into revealing his foreignness: he too is a member of an occupying ruling class (p. 563). Azdak thus seizes his moment.

By showing us the kind of man Azdak is—a basically goodhearted, idealistic person who uses his mordant wit as a defense against existent corruption and injustice—Brecht prepares us for the existentially opportune moment when revolutionary fortune makes his assuming the judgeship possible. With the previous judge's hanged corpse still present in the courtroom like the corpus on a crucifix, holding the eye, there can be no doubt of the price of failure, no question about the stakes involved. We can predict the nature of Azdak's judgeship from the brief glimpse given of his prior life: like Grusha, Azdak says one thing and does another—but in a manner quite opposite to what is done by mankind in general. Grusha complains, but does good; Azdak rationalizes, uses the statute books to sit upon, and accepts bribes—but he also *renders justice*, a thing unheard of. As the Story Teller's comments make clear, it is only in times of chaos that the poor—who have little to lose—stand a chance of gain:

> In the castle, fanatics. At the altar, heretics.
> And Azdak wearing a judge's gown.

(p. 564)

By assuming the burdens of both justice and mercy, Azdak combines the godlike attributes of Father *and* Son.

The sampling of Azdak's justice we are given (pp. 564-68) indicates the way in which his conception of justice applies to a cross-section of society (rather in the way the overall structure of the play permits each act to treat one member of a series of related topics: the state, the military, religion, etc.). An invalid is fined for investing in a doctor's career, while the doctor is acquitted of the crime of having forgotten his fee (Brecht's doctor-baiting runs all through the play); an innkeeper is fined for bringing a selfish legal action unnecessarily; and a gorgeous girl is convicted of "assault with a dangerous weapon" and thus rape. Again, the Story Teller moralizes, and this time it is clearly the Christian ethic the weaknesses of which—as Brecht sees them—are under scrutiny:

> All mankind should love each other but when visiting your
>   brother
> Take an axe along and hold it fast.
> Not in theory but in practice miracles are wrought with axes
> And the age of miracles is not past.

(p. 568)

Especially in its combination of brutal referents ("axes") and naive beliefs ("miracles"), Brecht's notion of revolutionary justice is obviously never without its element of simple force.

But it is in the case of the Old Woman (pp. 568-70) that Azdak most clearly supports a questionable "legality" as a force

66

to support goodness. Because she has lost a son in the war, she has been the recipient of stolen favours from a local Robin Hood, the bandit Irakli. Though Irakli enters the courtroom armed with the sort of ax we have just heard sung of, Azdak treats him cordially and accepts the Old Woman's vision of him as "Saint Banditus". Azdak even refers to her as, in effect, the spirit of his suffering nation, "Mother Grusinia the Woebegone", asking her "merciful verdict on Us the Damned". And because it takes a miracle for a poor old woman to find sustenance as she has—with the help of her "Saint"—Azdak then convicts the plaintiff farmers of atheism for their failure to "believe". As the Story Teller puts it, again in Christ-related imagery,

> Statute and rule he broke like a loaf to feed the folk.
> On the wreck of the law he brought them to the shore . . .
>
> (p. 570)

Before the reappearance of the Governor's wife reminding us of the pending case of Grusha and Michael, Azdak concludes that such an unnatural thing as justice can thrive only in what has already been called an "era of disorder".

In the final act (Part II, Section 2), The Chalk Circle demonstration is finally accomplished. Grusha is praying for luck in the court—a piece of business that equates her belief in that sort of prayer with superstition—though the Cook reassures her that "It's not a real judge. It's Azdak" (p. 574), and she is therefore already lucky. When Grusha meets the same Ironshirt Corporal whom she had knocked unconscious in order to save Michael, he refuses to recognize her—a parody of Peter's denial of Christ, but with opposite effects (pp. 575-76). Yet Adzak is the potential hanged/crucified here, and he is now dragged in, victim of the change in regimes. Beaten and kicked, like Christ, he asks for a rag (reminding one of Jesus on the Cross, asking for relief for his thirst), but it is in order to wipe the blood away (serving as his own Veronica) to see his enemies, whom he contemptuously calls "you dogs" (pp. 576-77). Azdak thus rejects the Christian expedient of meek cheek-turning, and still is saved (this side of death, and without need for a Resurrection) by the prompt arrival of a most theatrical messenger from the Grand Duke.

Now the beaten Azdak, so recently close to death, calls the

Ironshirts "fellow dogs" (p. 578), his sympathies having been honed even further. Grusha cannot even provide him with a widow's mite of a bribe, and will not perjure herself; but she does remind Azdak of the virtues of simplicity and ordinariness. Immediately thereafter, Azdak amuses himself by sparring with Simon in folk adages (pp. 581-82), agreeing that he knows his justice no better than a common soldier: "With me, everything goes for food and drink—I was educated at a convent" (p. 582). He baits Grusha until she waxes to a righteous indignation; calling him "the cracked Isaiah on the church window", she rises to a peak of forceful articulation (goodness responding positively to pressure, quite the opposite of Melville's Billy Budd) on behalf of justice, which is precisely what Azdak wants her to do (pp. 582-83). There is now a brief interruption for the comic interlude of the old couple who want a divorce, a device which both delays the ending of the play and makes possible the reuniting of Grusha and Simon—another parody of conventional comedic and religious values (pp. 583, 586). Asked by the judge whether she does not want Michael to "be rich", Grusha cannot find the words (she wants him to be good instead, the Story Teller says in her behalf); yet Azdak answers her silence, "I think I understand you, woman" (p. 584)—a particularly Christlike mode of address and demonstration of understanding. They have reached a plane of spiritual oneness that makes the Chalk Circle test simply a dramatic pretext, almost an afterthought.

Grusha being of course unwilling to hurt Michael during the two runs of the test, Azdak finds her the child's "true mother" (the improvement on sources mentioned earlier). The Governor's estates are confiscated to become a playground to be called Azdak's Garden—a foreshadowing of the Caucasian-land settlement—and Azdak himself resigns his office and declares that the trial, and thus the play, is to end like a Shakespearean or Restoration comedy—in a dance (pp. 585-86). As for Grusha, she reveals that she took Michael on that Easter Sunday because she had become engaged to Simon; now, still a virgin, she considers him the "child of love" of herself and the Joseph-like Simon (p. 586). Thus the play's religious values are encapsulated and concluded: Azdak has yielded his place, and will fade away from view during the dance, perhaps to become a dream of his people, an Arthur— the embodiment of a "brief golden age/ Almost an age of justice" (p. 587), as though such a thing were too much to hope for. Azdak is gone, perhaps to be replaced by Michael, who in agreement with the conventions of dramatic tradition represents the synthesis of father and mother, the ultimate Marxism of sex.

Yet in another sense, I think that Grusha bore this child— was given it—by Azdak, or by what he represented (love+force) as much as or more than by Simon. If Simon is a soldier, Azdak is something more: the type of the benign state Brecht envisaged, using its authority for the common good and not susceptible to venality. In this funny, earthy, human play so difficult to realize onstage in the totality of its intended effects, I would not claim a greater "Christian" presence than what I think Brecht intended—that is, as one of a series of myth-structures available for exploitation for didactic/ dramatic purposes, but especially as one which he might use to bait the "Christian" West. The issue of whether any state, particularly a socialist one, can in fact stand for the sort of secular Christianity posited by *The Caucasian Chalk Circle* strikes me as quite irrelevant to the issue at hand: whether Brecht's Azdak is successful as an embodiment of the Marxist-Christian ethic in the form of a dying King of the Year. Given a chance by a sympathetic stage production, Azdak will (it seems fair to predict, borrowing from Hopkins) successfully "easter in us" as he must.

NOTE

A version of this chapter first appeared in the American journal *The New Laurel Review,* with whose kind permission it is now reprinted here in revised form.

1   Bertolt Brecht, *The Caucasian Chalk Circle,* trans. Eric Bentley and Maja Apelman, in *Seven Plays by Bertolt Brecht* (New York, 1961). All page references appear parenthetically within my text.

6

Eliot's Christ of the Pattern: *Murder in the Cathedral*

Like Eugene O'Neill's *The Iceman Cometh,* T.S. Eliot's play *Murder in the Cathedral* (1935)[1] is one of those titles which comes to mind automatically when the possibility of a study of the Christ-theme in modern drama is raised. There is no avoiding dealing with either play. But whereas the Christ presence or myth in *Iceman* is diffused, communicated to more than one individual, in *Murder* it is intentionally concentrated: one man bears the burden of the office, and that by authorial election. Thomas à Becket becomes, at Eliot's hands, the man elected to renew the Waste Land, the Christ designed to refructify the desert place. Thus in many respects, *Murder* is a point of culmination in Eliot's career; answering the patent longing of the earlier works, it points the way for what is yet to come. Moreover, by acting as the successful starting-place for Eliot's verse-dramas, it marks what some would term a devolution into the positive.

The awareness with which Eliot presents Thomas as Christ-figure is, of course, quite critically inhibiting. I would hope to escape the more conventional routings by proceeding, false-naively, as though nothing previous had taken place, and by confronting the text anew. Nevertheless, it must be confessed initially that Eliot is not, as was the case with Strindberg, telling more than he knew; he was fully conscious of nearly every aspect of his chosen myth's operatings. But what I find most fascinating about Eliot's treatment of a given mythic pattern is the way in which he accepts the story of Jesus as precisely the

70

proper *mythos* for his Becket; I mean, for Eliot sainthood is exactly the imitation of Christ it has traditionally been defined to be, and the role of the playwright is an extension of this same creative function: to accept into one's life the implications of the mission of Jesus on earth. Thus Becket's assumption of the mantle of Christian leadership is paralleled by Eliot's artistry in recreating him. In Eliot's canon, then, the expectation of the Messiahship of Christ becomes an operative aesthetic norm, the fulfilment of a universal human need and the regeneration of a spiritual desert.

The process by which this theatrical enactment occurs is one which parallels, in several significant respects, the ritual of the Catholic Mass. Not only is the play divided into two "parts", not acts, with a sermon or homily in between, but those parts correspond to the Masses of the Catechumens and Faithful respectively: that is, there is a section devoted to textual explication, or exposition, followed by a demonstration, or sacrificial act. Futhermore, the poetic texts which Eliot creates to surround his actions are at certain points parallel to, or parodic of, the Ordinary and Proper of the Mass. All of this is seen as fulfilment of the year-cycle myth with which Eliot was early fascinated, but with a difference—the removal of the blockage of renewal by means of the sacrificial gesture already referred to. The conversion of the poet/playwright to the notion of a benign cyclicality is aided in presentation, moreover, by an operative device I shall call the three-plus-one. Through this device, implications of historical finality are evaded, and assumptions of inevitability are escaped, as the threes of fatality and "rightness" are replaced by a figure expressing harmony to the human consciousness—the square which replaces the harsh angularities of the triangle.

Eliot does this by suggesting that human actions can make a difference, and that eternal patterns can be freely accepted, and positively, in a way which dispenses with the doom inherent in a pagan conception of the human condition, especially in classic Greek drama. Such a concept will please or displease the audience member depending on his/her own predilections, of course, but for the vestigial Christian it will make sense to define free will in terms of the accepting of divine Will. Thus a play with all the trappings of Greek tragedy is deliberately robbed of

71

its strict tragic finality; Christian hope is seen triumphant at the end, and human doubtings are replaced by certitude. In the process, Eliot forces the audience to choose between the ordinarily human and the especial, the saintly; in Eliot's view of things, the choice requires little deliberation, once the individual has witnessed the demonstration called *Murder in the Cathedral*.

Murder in the Cathedral: the very title is at war with itself, and creates for the thoughtful listener the central conflict between an instinct for safety at all costs—a human, or perhaps more accurately, animal instinct as Eliot presents it—and the willingness to be more fully human because allowing the operation of the divine within oneself. Such an operation is little like the Nietzschean/Ibsenian/Shavian/Strindbergian notions of Will or Life Force in action, but rather more like the traditional Christian concept of grace. To accept its working, the individual opens himself/herself to an inflooding divinity, but in the process puts self in mortal danger. This is the Christ who came to bring a sword: earthly unease is the price of eternal sainthood. In such a way, the title of the play sums up the contradictions in terms which its action resolves. How can there be murder in the cathedral, we ask; danger in the place of sanctuary? Is not a cathedral a place of refuge from the world without?

Precisely this issue is faced by the Women of Canterbury in their opening choral ode:

> Here let us stand, close by the cathedral. Here let us wait.
> Are we drawn by danger? Is it the knowledge of safety, that
> draws our feet
> Towards the cathedral? What danger can be
> For us, the poor, the poor women of Canterbury? what
> tribulation
> With which we are not already familiar? There is no danger
> For us, and there is no safety in the cathedral. Some presage of
> an act
> Which our eyes are compelled to witness, has forced our feet
> Towards the cathedral. We are forced to bear witness.
>
> (p. 11)

What "forces" the ordinary poor towards the dangerous place is, in effect, what brings the pilgrims in Chaucer's verse-tale there two centuries later: the unfolding drama of Thomas à Becket's martyrdom. Though the ordinary poor cannot in fact participate in this drama, except as onookers, their roles are not without significance. They react to oncoming events with the trepidation of animals, the instincual excitement felt by the servant Dunyasha at the beginning of *The Cherry Orchard,* once she knows the Ranevskys are coming home. The unrelenting power of drama, similarly, has placed us in our audience chairs—or pews—and we are "forced to bear witness" though we, like Prufrock, are not of heroic stature ourselves. Such a placement does not imply, strictly speaking, a voyeuristic interest in what is about to happen; rather, it is a testimonial to the inherent ability of powerful drama to attract us, even against our reasonable and prudential assumptions.

The "danger" being referred to has as its origin the threat of intrusion of the outside world into the sanctuary of the cathedral, as I have mentioned already in passing. In fact, that intrusion is central to Eliot's purposes, for his drama rests upon its impact, and his presentation of ideas is wholly concerned with its meaning. For Eliot is explicitly concerned with the dangers to religion of official establishment: the ironic menace of governmental preferment and "protection" of one faith as against another. In Eliot's view, the Established Church in England has suffered an historical withering-away for no other reason than its own officially recognized status as *the* English Church. Like a forced marriage, then, the Church-state relationship has made possible a sort of rape, accomplished in this play by the phallic swords' points of the four assassin knights. Thus the safety of the Church's position in English life, although theoretically legally assured, is a deception and a hoax: it is a license to die. By moving his play into the cathedral, Eliot was making sure that his audiences understood, and responded accordingly.

And by moving the play into the cathedral—indeed, to this day the play continues to be performed amazingly often in church structures around the world—Eliot was able to remind that audience that Christ did truly come to bring a sword, and that the progress of a Christian could not be easy. As well, *Murder* reminds us of what university professors are fond of assuring their students: that Western drama was reborn in the churches, and that what we recognise as the heritage of Western dramatic tradition had its origins in the performance of lines from the Easter liturgy. By its very rootship, therefore, our theatre is "religious" and centred on the fact of the Resurrection; and no matter how muddled those sources become to the average audience member watching a Neil Simon comedy, the historical fact remains that our drama springs from the recelebration of the death and rebirth of the Christ. The striking paradox here is that a Redeemer who brought one kind of sword would perish by another kind; but the resolution of that paradox is even more impressive, for it involves the miraculous transcending of the necessity for living with the expectation of a permanent defeat.

It is this triumph over linear fatality that Eliot uses to connect his plot with the celebration of the myth of the year: its death, and its rekindling. Thus although Eliot has neither the salient features of the Christian calendar to work with, both the beginning of Advent and Eastertide being denied him by historical accident, he does have the great fact of the ending of the secular calendar year to play upon. Thus he is able to manipulate the psychological yearnings for renewal of a mankind at the ending of another twelvemonth ordeal. He can therefore pretend that his play's climax, and that of the Church year he consistently reminds us of, are coincidental. The cyclicality of the natural year, then, can function as a source of hope in Eliot's play, quite the opposite of the way it suggests defeat in later Absurdist drama. And what causes the year to "move" again, of course, is the presence of its appropriate superhuman sacrifice, the deed of blood and faith felt lacking in the early poems, and therefore producing no movement, no salvation.

Accordingly, the Chorus immediately moves into a consideration of the movements of the seasons in Nature. "The New Year waits, breathes, whispers in darkness" (p. 11), we are told, and an anticipatory excitement takes over its utterance, imaged in Nature. This habit of referring to Nature's moods, of course, is not Eliot's invention, but another borrowing from the Greeks; but in his hands it becomes Christianised, merged most neatly with the deeds of "saints and martyrs" which are the notches of the gears which move the Christian year along. An invocation to December wonders at the "Destiny" that "waits in the hand of God":

> Come, happy December, who shall observe you, who shall
>   preserve you?
> Shall the Son of Man be born again in the litter of scorn?
> For us, the poor, there is no action,
> But only to wait and to witness.
>
> (p. 13)

Thus the awaiting, the role to which the poor are consigned, is simultaneously directed towards the possibility of another Christ's coming and to the absence of the good Archbishop.

This identification of Thomas and Christ is confirmed, and speedily, by the language and action of the play. The First Priest refers to Thomas, in terms of the poor, as "their friend, their Father in God" (p. 14), in a context of Thomas's imminence. And immediately, as if by Ibsenian cue, a Messenger brings news of Thomas's arrival in England— though as the First Priest makes clear by his inquiry, there is quite a difference between coming "in full assurance" and coming "only secure/In the power of Rome, the spiritual rule,/The assurance of right, and the love of the people" (pp. 14-15). Love and right are not enough to protect Thomas, then; but for the moment he is welcomed by crowds who in their "frenzied enthusiasm" are "Lining the road and throwing down their capes,/Strewing the way with leaves and late flowers of the season" (p. 15). Here is a concrete example of Eliot's manipulation of the secular and ecclesiastical years, for the clearly described offstage scene makes Thomas's return an event in Nature that recalls by its differences the entry of Christ into Jerusalem. The very hair of the tail of Thomas's horse, it is suggested with some dryness, is about to become a relic, but we are told as soon that Thomas has parted from the King of France in the apparent certainty of his coming end (p. 16). Meanwhile, the scene onstage is one of patent preparedness for the coming of a theatrical event, one which is unapologized for by much in the way of naturalistic justifications. Thomas is coming, as rapidly as spring in *Caucasian Chalk Circle,* and we are waiting for an Entrance. That is all.

But before Thomas arrives, the priests discuss him, and while the First Priest draws attention to Thomas's historical state of being "isolated" and "insecure" among Henry's courtiers, the Second Priest refers to Thomas as a "rock" on whom they can all rely: "The rock of God is beneath our feet" (pp. 17-18). Thus in one exchage of opinions, Thomas has been presented in putatively tragic aloneness and yet as congruent with the Church, the rock, which he speaks for. Both situations spring from Thomas's closeness to God, and by the latter image we are reminded that in this play, the "house" in which the action of the play takes place is the House of God, a church; and not just any church, but a cathedral, which acquires its special nature from the bishop assigned there. Thus Thomas is equivalent to a cathedral, a church, in this play; and by corollary the stage set, or church, if that is where the play is performed, is the outward dramatic realization of Thomas's inward state. The danger which threatens this individual man, from without and within, is therefore equated with the danger to the institutional Church generally.

Thomas has nearly arrived, but it is necessary for the Third Priest to introduce still another dramatic metaphor for our consideration before he gets here. It is that of the "wheel", the ongoing mechanism of change—not precisely equivalent to the standard definition of the medieval conception of Fortune's wheel on which we almost predictably rise and then fall, but rather the mysterious cosmic device by which God's Will is made manifest throughout the universe. "For good or ill, let the wheel turn" (p. 18), says the Third Priest; and yet this is itself not equivalent to the Brechtian notion (seen in *Caucasian Chalk Circle* and elsewhere) that for the poor, any change means hope, since the poor have nothing to lose. For Eliot's poor "do not wish anything to happen," content with their half-lives, their eventless existences:

> O Thomas, return, Archbishop; return, return to France.
> Return. Quickly. Quietly. Leave us to perish in quiet.
> You come with applause, you come with rejoicing, but you
>   come bringing death into Canterbury:
> A doom on the house, a doom on yourself, a doom on the
>   world.

                                                     (pp. 18-19)

House, self, world—the equations acknowledged by the Chorus

are those which share in Thomas's "doom", no merely private happening, surely. And can a Thomas understand what it means to be "the small folk drawn into the pattern of fate", "The strain on the brain of the small folk who stand to the doom" thus expected (pp. 18-21)?

Apparently he can, for he enters chiding the Second Priest who would have the Chorus put on a "pleasant" public face with which to greet their Archbishop. Thomas's first word, in fact, is a Christlike "Peace", once the second Priest has given him an M.C.'s sort of introduction; but his following speech indicates that peace is Thomas's prayer, not his expectation. Given the reference to "applause" and the manner of Thomas's coming-on, it is not surprising that Eliot has Thomas get right down to business, no nonsense and no naturalistic small talk. Indeed, Thomas launches immediately into what we later deduce to be an important revelation of his inner state:

> They know and do not know, what it is to act or suffer
> They know and do not know, that action is suffering
> And suffering is action. Neither does the agent suffer
> Nor the patient act. But both are fixed
> In an eternal action, an eternal patience
> To which all must consent that it may be willed
> And which all must suffer that they may will it,
> That the pattern may subsist, for the pattern is the action
> And the suffering, that the wheel may turn and still
> Be forever still.
>
> (pp. 21-2)

Thomas's reconciliation of semantic opposites is more a crossing of Christian apologetics and Yeatsian cosmology than anything the listeners of the historical Becket might have understood, but its poet's play with notions of action and suffering does manage to create an eye-of-God identity between the perfect act (the imitation of God, who in Thomistic terms is pure Act), that is, acceptance of divine will by conscious affirmation, and perfect suffering, the ultimate meaning of that curious religio-historical term, the Passion. Thomas has reasoned himself into a sphere of thought in which distinctions between active and passive verbs become linguistic tricks.

No time is wasted, therefore, in getting the "meanings" of this play out before the audience. "End will be simple, sudden,

God-given", Thomas predicts; and he continues to deal with old familiar Eliotish oppositions of shadow and act. Indeed, Thomas puns on "act" in referring to this portion of events, or of the play, as "our first act" the substance of which "Will be shadows, and the strife with shadows". These shadows will shortly appear on stage, for Thomas's enemies are self-indictingly less than fully human persons, and they dwell in the world of illusions, while Thomas has the heightened clarity of vision of the illuminated. "Heavier the interval than the consummation", he intones; "All things prepare the event. Watch" (p. 23). Thus Thomas, as deftly as Christ at his own Last Supper, manages a theatrical event, even doling out cues to those who think they have him in their power. And it is according to Thomas's own cueing that the First Tempter enters, though clearly the latter thinks he is barging in upon Thomas's attention without "ceremony" (p. 24).

Now it is perfectly obvious that Eliot has graded his characters beforehand in terms of their moral significances, for only Thomas speaks in sheer poetry, though the choral passages contain flights of gorgeous language as well. But the sympathy between Thomas and the poor accounts for this. Priests and Messenger speak in competent verse, while the Tempters talk in doggerel and (I would think this is meant to be conveyed through manner of delivery, for the lines are not in themselves totally objectionable at times) a clichéd, salesman's poetry. First Tempter, for example, offers Thomas memories of a possibly non-existent past and glimpses of an unlikely future. Thomas rejects them out of hand, but their importance is not to be overlooked: they represent the safer alternatives to living in the existential Now which in Chekhov are the indulgence of all his characters, and which Eugene O'Neill's characters will term "pipe dreams" even as they light up. My point here is that this first temptation is, like its successors, expressed in smarmy speech which is the self-indictment of its speaker. And of course, the Knights of Part II, when they appear (this is particularly important when the Tempters double as the Knights), speak politicians' prose. Sub-prose, *sub rosa*. It is interesting to note that Eliot's version of the singular escape possible, in the view of creative writers from Ibsen through Sartre and into the present moment, that is, the becoming oneself of a creative artist, is represented by Thomas, the incipient saint, attaining to genuine poetic power: a major voice of the twentieth century operating at the peak of his craft, and speaking as his major character. Presumably a Thomas à Becket, deprived of the opportunity of martyrdom by contemporary circumstances, might opt to become his namesake, a Thomas Stearns Eliot.

In Thomas's answer to First Tempter, we find revealed a peculiar adaptation of Christian tradition in the matter of Free Will. For Thomas rejects the temptation to return to the past, the lure of nostalgia, by claiming that "Only/ The fool, fixed in his folly, may think/ He can turn the wheel on which he turns" (p. 25). The implication, if I may refine it a bit, is that departures from acceptance of divine Will constitute folly, which seems acceptable enough; but folly not merely because it is foolish to err against the perfect order of things, but also because such behaviour is ineffective, and has no results. I leave the matter to theologians, with only the final observation that Eliot wishes to impose upon Thomas a Christlike obeisance to divine Will that implies something of Christlike awareness of what that Will might be. Small wonder Thomas is distanced from the other men at court. Moreover, Thomas's objection to the idea of meaningful change is itself opposed to the course of action he has taken, one which is surely expected to make chages for the better in human hearts.

First Tempter retreats with a resumption of doggerel, while Thomas concludes that "The impossible" is a lure into a "dead world,/ So that the mind may not be whole in the present" (pp. 26-7). Therefore Second Tempter approaches Thomas in just these terms: Take the reins of real power now, he advises, lest you waste yourself contending with shadows. This Tempter has learned one possible route into Thomas's soul—suggesting how much good he could accomplish in the world of real decision-making: "Power is present, for him who will wield" (pp. 28-9). This is, of course, the Shavian argument, the one on which *Major Barbara* rests its case; but Thomas will have none of a power lesser than the one he says he already possesses:

Temporal power, to build a good world,
To keep order, as the world knows order.

(p. 31)

Thomas's scorn is premised on Eliot's social conservatism, and one notes how contemporary an issue is being examined here, how "relevant" to present-day Church affairs.

Well, temptations come in threes, as anyone who has read the New Testament knows. Thomas has expected his Third Tempter, though the Second has involved him enough to participate with him in an exchange of ballad-like question-and-answer speech. Third Tempter comes on as a rough-and-ready pragmatist, and he offers Thomas the temptation of faction—of joining the barons against the King, at least temporarily: "To make, then break", as Thomas puts it. but Thomas will have none of a temptation to treason against his king; not only is the Caesar-God dichotomy of responsibilities operative here, but the king is in his sphere of proper action as supreme as the authority on which Thomas's exercise of power rests for its justification. The course of unprincipled political improvisation is thus also rejected (pp. 32-7), with Thomas citing Samson as an example of failing power exercised in desperation.

Now the Fourth Tempter enters, nameless and to Thomas's surprise. Christ had three tempters, and such things come in threes; this is a ritual drama which is taking place, so why should there be a Fourth? Fourth Tempter, however, presents a posture to which Jesus was presumably prevented from attraction by his dual nature—the inner temptation to play the God, to *want* the cup that will not pass away. You are going to die, says the Fourth Tempter; why not embrace your death for the sake of the "spiritual power" it will bring you? It is "the keys of heaven and hell" that Thomas holds, "The thread of eternal life and death" (p. 39): "Saint and Martyr rule from the tomb" (p. 40). Perhaps because Thomas à Becket is the clearest example of a Christ-figure in modern drama, especially as consciously presented by the playwright, it is necessary for Eliot to show that Thomas is *not* in fact the Christ. Christlike, he faces the additional burden of risking his life for the sake of a memory among men that may not last; for when "the wheel turns" again, as the Tempter puts it, there will come a time of irreligion and then, worse yet, an age of psychological rationalization, of scholarly debunking of the great:

And later is worse, when men will not hate you

Enough to defame or to execrate you,
But pondering the qualities that you lacked
Will only try to find the historical fact.
When men shall declare that there was no mystery
About this man who played a certain part in history.

(p. 41)

Of course, this is precisely the thrust of Thomas's own thinking
and the drift of his doubting, and the Tempter meets his initial
refusals by deftly quoting Thomas's own earlier remarks upon
action and suffering (p. 43). Thomas has already termed this
desire to die for God "Dreams to damnation" (p. 43), for in this
play hell is the place of illusions, where tempters have their
proper abode, but this Fourth Tempter must be seen to have
caused Thomas to reel backwards in self-doubt. Tempter's last
words, ". . . that the wheel may turn and still/ Be forever still",
now lack the clever effect of Thomas's reading, for the Chorus
responds—Thomas having been quite silenced—by picking up
the word "still" and developing the theme of social unease:

There is no rest in the house. There is no rest in the street.
I hear restless movement of feet. And the air is heavy and
thick.
Thick and heavy the sky. And the earth presses up against our
feet.

(p. 43)

—and so on, expressing like a Brechtian storyteller the torment
Thomas is going through, and which must be seen in the actions
and expressions of the actor playing Thomas. Indeed, the
cataclysmic nature of the Fourth Tempter's thrust can be seen
by its dramatic results. For one, the Chorus casts Thomas forth
in time, speaking anachronistically of life's disappointments,
including a capsule lifetime of things which turn out to have
been less than they promised to be:

The Catherine wheel, the pantomime cat,
The prizes given at the children's party,
The prize awarded for the English Essay,
The scholar's degree, the statesman's decoration.
All things become less real, man passes
From unreality to unreality.

(p. 44)

81

And thus the Chorus presses home the charge that Thomas is himself lost in the "final illusion" of his "own greatness", followed by the Priests' choral passage advising inaction (p. 44).

And more. A triple choral assault now begins, Chorus, Priests and Tempters each taking a line and driving it home. The gist of these passages (pp. 44-5), which are quite telling in their chilling beauty, is the universal human apprehensiveness in the presence of Death. Thereafter, the Chorus of Women takes advantage of Thomas's shaken state to speak of its own sort of suffering, speaking ironically with the tired wisdom of the lifelong poor: "We have not been happy, my Lord, we have not been too happy./ . . ." (p. 45). "God is leaving us", they intone, and the implication is that Thomas, their "Lord", takes faith and hope with him if he deserts his flock; their pleas that he save them by saving himself seem to have the effect of wresting Thomas out of his Gethsemane of doubt, for his next speech is filled with resumed authority and decisiveness:

> Now is my way clear, now is the meaning plain;
> Temptation shall not come in this kind again.
> The last temptation is the greatest treason:
> To do the right deed for the wrong reason.
>
> (p. 47)

By using the word "treason", Thomas makes clear a parallel between his own stewardship for King Henry and his responsibilities towards himself—i.e., towards his Maker. As Thomas would not betray his King, acting as spritual Lord, he would not let his corporeal part be betrayed by the spiritual—a prideful soul that might crave martyrdom, and thus "do the right deed for the wrong reason". Now he can confidently face his audience—ourselves—and declare that while they, we, may say that what he is doing is "at best futility,/ Senseless self-slaughter of a lunatic,/ Arrogant passion of a fanatic", there is to be no evasion of moral responsibility here, no clever diplomacy about who must bear the blame for what. By having Thomas speak directly to his previously unacknowledged second audience (beyond that of our surrogate-selves, the Chorus of the Women of Canterbury), Eliot ends Part I of his play by not only a theatricality that leaves us buzzing in the intermission, but also incorporates our presences into the body of the Faithful who are to witness, who *must* witness, what is yet to transpire (p. 48). It is for us that the sacrifice is to take place.

And now, just at the point in a Roman Mass where a sermon or homily would be delivered, Eliot has Thomas give his Christmas message to his Canterbury congregation (pp. 51-4). It is curious indeed that the Anglo-Catholic Eliot should make his play resemble a Roman service more than an Anglican one, but I think his motivations may be more than historical fidelity to Becket's times. What the play preaches—since we are at the point in it where Thomas preaches—is Disestablishment, the independence of the English Church. Thus whatever serves to sever the ties which make the English Church an arm of the civil government advances, in Eliot's eyes, its holiness, integrity, and Englishness. A paradox is therefore born: to the degree that the Church of Becket's day, and presumably our own, is "Roman", that is, fully autonomous, it is correspondingly and healthily "English". An interesting state of affairs, but then, it would be like this expatriate American to attempt a one-man twentieth-century Oxford Movement of his own.

That Christmas message, not unexpectedly, combines certain of Eliot's preoccupations in one brief oration. First, the Christian year is folded upon itself as Thomas reminds his hearers of the relationship between the Nativity and Easter (pp. 51-3); mourning and rejoicing are forever joined together in the Christian consciousness. One means of accomplishing this is to point out that the feast of the first martyr, St. Stephen, follows the feast of Chrismas by one day. This device cues the more aware members of the audience to the reflection on the particular Church usage known as daily propers that is to follow, including reference to the aforesaid St. Stephen—stoned by the people of Jerusalem, as Thomas is to be murdered in a city clearly parelleled with Jerusalem in the play, given its central importance to the English Church. The message here is simple: to accept Christ as a model means, in effect, to accept his death for oneself, even literally. Martyrs, like Christ, are to be mourned and rejoiced over at once; but it is to be remembered that "a Christian martyrdom is never an accident", but rather "is always the design of God", not man, and therefore never anything less than a gesture by one who "has lost his will in the will of God, and who no longer desires anything for himself, not even the glory of being a martyr." So that as Thomas prepares for his own coming death, quite clearly predicted by the end of the sermon, we have the unusual situation of a play's having reached its point of clear and final self-exposition when it is scarcely halfway through. But that is in the nature of both communal religious celebration and orthodox tragedy, as Eliot perceives it.

Part II is that communal religious celebration, one which involves pre-Christian allusions to the death of the year-king, the myth with which the early Eliot poetry is so obsessed. For the Chorus has been noting the effects in Nature of Thomas's arrival and spiritual dilemma, and this new section begins with a choral utterance specifically devoted to the signs of unease in the world around Canterbury. No signs of spring are apparent, but only the increasing evidence of a dead year—this despite the passing of the winter solstice, and the theoretical lengthening of days which should follow:

> The peace of this world is always uncertain, unless men keep
>   the peace of God.
> And war among men defiles this world, but death in the Lord
>   renews it. . .
>
>   (p. 57)

The end of the year has sullied the world, but death will clean it, the Chorus tells us; and the peace which Thomas proffered on his first appearance is only to be attained in terms of accommodation with divine wishes, that is to say, by means of the death of Thomas himself. Waiting remains the dramatic keynote.

By means of the banners they bear and the texts they recite, the Three Priests now enter with the reminder that three feast days follow the feast of Christmas and precede the death of Thomas—the feasts of St. Stephen, St. John the Apostle, and the Holy Innocents. But Eliot interweaves these feasts with his major themes by having the Priests recite language which imitates the Mass propers for those feast days, according to the Roman missal (pp. 58-9). But whether Roman missal or Book of Common Prayer, the point of all this ritual is both to make the sacrifice of Thomas congruent with Church usage, and also to

84

confirm another instance of the three-plus-one. For Three Priests bring their banners, reminding us of three feast days after Christmas, but the killing of Thomas takes place on 29 December: "Since the Holy Innocents a day: the fourth day from Christmas," as the First Priest puts it (p. 59). "What is to-day?" they ask in turn, this fourth day after Christmas? It is the day when, to cite another text just quoted in the play, "He lays down his life for the sheep" (p. 60). It is the day of the Fourth Priest, Thomas; 29 December is to be his feast day for all time to come, and this play and the tableau it is about to present is his "banner".

Yet to ordinary men, the chosen day is seldom clearly that; only "in retrospection, selection", do we recognize it as the day on which "The eternal design" appeared, and even then the design is obscured "in sordid particulars" (pp. 60-1). Possibly punning on particulars, Eliot has the Four Knights enter immediately upon this cue; the banners are taken away, and the nature of the dramatic moment changes abruptly and in a stylized manner, as it might in the observance of a ritual event (p. 61). Their threatening nature, as they decline the hospitality of the Priests under the press of their "business", is clear enough to Thomas as he returns onstage. Yet even he is unprepared for the exact moment of his ending, although he had put all his affairs in order in expectation of some such occurrence one of these days (pp. 62-3). Curiously enough, one aspect of the Knights' enmity, as it appears in the joint accusation of the first Three Knights, is wrath at Thomas's low birth; only in this respect does Eliot seem to wish to indicate a natural complicity between Eliot and the women of the Chorus, and that is perhaps in order to indicate a proportionality in their relationship and in that of king and subjects. Naturally enough, such a proportionality is supported by Biblical evidence: Christ is always "Lord", God "King", etc. (p. 64).

A certain amount of taunting irony follows (pp. 64-5), the Knights resembling Christ's Roman soldiers in this regard. Further New Testament allusions appear as the priests make to interpose themselves between Thomas and his attackers, but Thomas rejects assistance: it is time (p. 67). Thus by moving backwards in the Passion narrative to the scene of Jesus's arrest in the midst of his disciples, Eliot conveys a sense of having

85

telescoped the Passion narrative drastically; the accusations made against Thomas, following immediately, are reminiscent of Jesus's trials, but the resemblances are by no means so pronounced as to warrant my making much of them. The situation speaks for itself, however; Thomas stands in clear stead, surrogate for divine will (p. 70), refusing to acknowledge the flattery of personal attacks. For Thomas has surrendered his own ego to a higher purpose, one which he promises to "rise from my tomb" to lay his cause before (p. 71). By this means, the poet/playwright comes as close as possible to letting his human protagonist emulate the prophecy and fulfilment of his resurrection ascribed to Jesus—in the process strengthening the parallel between the two figures to the limits of plausibility.

The choral ode which follows is striking in the starkness of its imagery of corruption and death in nature; unlike Thomas, the Chorus stands self-accused of being "United to the spiritual flesh of nature,/ Mastered by the animal powers of spirit,/ Dominated by the lust of self-demolition,/ By the final utter uttermost death of spirit,/ By the final ecstasy of waste and shame . . ." (p. 74). In this Shakespearean language, the chorus allies itself with a lesser sort of eternal pattern—the purely physical, the pathetic fallacy (common also to Shakespeare) by which upset in human affairs is mirrored in lesser forms:

> What is woven on the loom of fate
> What is woven in the councils of princes
> Is woven also in our veins, our brains,
> Is woven like a pattern of living worms
> In the guts of the women of Canterbury.
>
> (p. 73)

The "pattern" of divine Will which Thomas is accepting to his death and his glory becomes, in the eyes of the "audience" of women who are our surrogate presences onstage, a debased concept of "fate" for which the proper image is "worms/ In the guts"—a movement upwards for the one, in other words, and downwards for the others. Yet Thomas promises the Chorus a "share of the eternal burden,/ The perpetual glory" (p. 74). The completion of God's purposes will eventually "pierce" them "with a sudden painful joy", but meanwhile a dreamlike oblivion will overtake them and deprive them of the anguish of fully conscious awareness of what is going on: "Human kind cannot bear very much reality" (p. 75). It is the enduring wisdom of much of modern drama that the confrontation with reality kills, while the illusion comforts and sustains life. But life sustained beyond the confrontation with reality is a sort of death-in-life, and thus tragic. Eliot agrees, but with the Christian proviso—or alternative—of becoming more nearly divine, and thus transcending the human dilemma. For Thomas, sainthood turns tragedy into triumph.

And so to that end, the priests, like frightened disciples of Christ, urge Thomas towards the altar and safety (though the altar is the place for the enactment of sacrifice), but Thomas demurs:

> No life here is sought for but mine,
> And I am not in danger: only near to death.
>
> (p. 75)

It is the attitude of a man both resigned and committed, but more: that of a man who is confident of ultimate salvation, and uses his confidence to reassure his followers:

> Go to vespers, remember me at your prayers.
> They shall find the shepherd here; the flock shall be spared.
> I have had a tremor of bliss, a wink of heaven, a whisper,
> And I would no longer be denied; all things
> Proceed to a joyful consummation.
>
> (p. 76)

Though the priests drag Thomas into the cathedral, it is to no earthly safety; but Thomas has already expressed his anticipatory pleasure at his heavenly reward in terms of quasi-sexual, or at least sensual, pleasure, the mystic's harmony of spiritual and physical "bliss". Or is the playwright even thinking in terms of some Teilhardian Omega-point?

It is time for the last Chorus episode before the death of Thomas, and it is appropriately death-centred. Moreover, the gist of the passage (pp. 76-8) is that Thomas is about to be sacrificed for the common good, for the return of rain to the dry Waste Land, for the appeasing of a wrathful God. While the *Dies Irae* is sung, the Chorus imitates the stanzaic pattern of that ancient hymn, as well as its emotional fright. Death is viewed as "God's silent servant", and the "Judgement" it leads to masks a "Void" which is "absence, separation from God", the Waste Land, the hell of modern theological definition. In short, it is the place where there is no escaping the truth:

> Where the soul is no longer deceived, for there are no objects,
> no tones,
> No colours, no forms to distract, to divert the soul
> From seeing itself, foully united forever, nothing with nothing,
> Not what we call death, but what beyond death is not death,
> We fear, we fear . . .

(p. 77)

Compare these lines with Hamlet's soliloquy. And note that at the end, the Chorus even adopts a rhyme scheme which alludes—through its differences with that of the wrathful *Dies Irae*, to which it is stanzaically similar, arguably—to a more hopeful prayer sequence, the *Stabat Mater*, wherein the focus is on redemption through the Cross of Jesus. In fact, precisely that is what the Chorus is begging during the passage in question (p. 78). After it, Thomas demands that the cathedral doors be opened, even though his Priests have just finished celebrating their achievement of safety behind the stone walls of the institutional church, or Church. Understanding their leader no better than Christ's apostles, they persist in setting their sights on temporary and earthly goals; Thomas's reply is to play, as Christ did, upon the nature of the Church as rock-established and lasting: it lasts, he says, because of its spirituality, not through "oak and stone", which both decay (p. 78).

Thomas explains his mission as one of obeisance to a power out of time, expecting that its worth will be judged in just such terms (p. 79). The beasts, the Knights, whom the Priests warn him of are already conquered, for the beasts he speaks of are within us: "We have only to conquer/ Now, by suffering. This is the easier victory" (p. 80). Acknowledging that his coming end is also "the triumph of the Cross"—i.e., a victory through a Passion—he causes the doors to be opened. He has already spoken of his coming death as a "consummation", a choice of terms which echoes Christ's description of the finished process of his own death on the Cross; and now the drunken Knights extend the comparison backwards, to Daniel, as they invite the latter-day prophet and interpreter of dreams down "to the lions' den" (p. 80). Like many of the other playwrights surveyed here, Eliot makes reference to unheeded prophecies which then require sacrificial acts, deeds of blood, by which the Christian witness adopts the role of sacrificial Lamb, if necessary—the ultimate emulation of the Christ.

His blood for Christ's, Thomas is ready for death: "That his Church may have peace and liberty" (p. 81). He makes his final deposition in terms familiar from the Roman Mass's Canon, and from its initial prayer of repentance. The killing of Thomas which follows, judging by the amount of time accorded to it—it is meant to occur as the Chorus chants a lengthy ode on the subject of defilement and the necessity for cleansing, purgation—is the occasional act of restoration which Eliot feels (one may assume) that the earth requires. Presumably, the world is still in need of such martyrs; Eliot almost seems to pick up Shaw's *St. Joan* and its Epilogue here, with its theme of the abiding need for fresh acts of sacrifice, fresh blood, to appease the need created by a wanton world. Thus the three-plus-one theme is abetted by Thomas's death—still another death is needed to complete, to square, the historical angularity of the chain of redemption for which Christ provided the example. Left with an earth of stones and dry places, the Chorus characterizes the world as "wholly foul", and in need of a thorough cleansing of its filth (pp. 82-3). I leave to others the psychological interpretation of this aspect of Eliot's pet obsessions, but note in passing that it takes nearly three pages of play text for the killing of Thomas to be accomplished.

It is therefore no casual homicide, this killing of the Archbishop; it is done with due ceremony instead of dispatch, and it forces us the audience to contemplate its meanings. From a consideration of the play as a whole, let us focus instead on this particular incident—one on which the play rests for meanings, and one at which a quasi-naturalistic action gives full way to something more nearly expressionistic, or something wholly other. At once a frozen moment of a chilling beauty, it is also an emblem of faith, a holy picuture for future generations; stained-glass window through which the actions of present and past times can be viewed, it is also a screen with holy things upon it, an iconostasis. Like the moment of *est* in the Roman Mass, it is a holy instant of transfiguration, of transubstantiation nearly. By it, the Christian purpose is renewed, and the titular paradox of murder in a place of sanctuary is resolved. Such earthly safety is rejected in favour of more permanent, eternal calm. We re-create it on our altar-stages; it sanctifies our acts.

We shall return to it later. For now, we note in passing that it ends the action of the play, allowing the Knights to step forward and address the audience directly—parodying Thomas's doing the same at the end of Part I. Perhaps it is revealing that the Fourth Knight, he who best knows Thomas's inner mind, speaks merely to advance the action of the play (p. 63); he is thus Thomas's unwitting accomplice. Afterwards, the Knights attempt to involve the audience in their deed, assuming complicity in a deed wrought for civic purposes, and in behalf of good British patriotism; reading complicity in the faces of the audience, they speak mock-piously of their having to arrive at "a just subordination of the pretensions of the Church to the welfare of the State" (pp. 84-8). Cranmer is cited, just to make sure it is seen that the episcopal shoe can be on the other foot as well. Still, Fourth Knight keeps silence.

But then the function of Fourth Knight, in this pattern of three-plus-one, is to represent the present day and its obsessions, justifications, and readings-in. He it is who, in the welter of political sub-prose, represents the modernist point of view, the tendency to explain away whatever upsets us. "Suicide while of Unsound Mind", he asks us to render as verdict (p. 90), paying homage to Thomas's onetime greatness in passing. Thus the Fourth Knight's statement is the most insidious of all, for it would explain away the spiritual value of Thomas's commitment. After the audience is urged to go quietly to their homes, the deliberations of the Priests resume.

The question is: Has the church been weakened, or renewed, by these events we have witnessed? *Renewed* is the apparent answer: there shall be an "oasis" in the desert, whereas the Knights are consigned to a living hell of perpetual make-believe. Thus Thomas is to be numbered with the company of the saints, and the Waste Land is to be considered renewed, watered with the blood of a new martyr. It is interesting to note that the final choral utterance is recited to a background chanting of the *Te Deum*, for by this act of Thomas's, a Requiem

Mass has been turned into a Mass of Thanksgiving. A victory is to be celebrated (pp. 92-4), and by it the "common man" is to be redeemed—that sub-species which is personified as a choral individual in Robert Bolt's *A Man for All Seasons*. Such men are all of us, and we share in the act by which the Chorus, at the end, takes the guilt for Thomas's death upon itself, much as the people of Jerusalem accepted the guilt for Christ's crucifixion. And finally, this act of repentance is augmented by the formal joining of Thomas to the company of the Elect: the Mass's Kyrie is increased by another line, and the pleas to "Lord" and "Christ" are added to by the name of "Blessed Thomas" (p. 94). It is as if another star had entered the skies, another constellation been born. Three-plus-one becomes the format of Eliot's play, but it also resolves the oddity of Biblical threesomes: a fourth is always needed to create a perfect form, a cross, say—like the cruciform churches of England, in the side of one of which Thomas à Becket was put to death, and where his blood poured forth.

Murder in the Cathedral, as it resolves the paradoxical implications of its title, is the replacement of the apparent mission of Christianity—as it has been taken to be in England, and elsewhere—with its real purpose: the bringing of the Sword of contention which makes of this life a struggle, the one to come an earned pacific state. For those who reject the bargain, the demonstration of the play is a patent fraud. For those who accept it, perhaps the play is quite unnecessary. For those who, like Eliot himself, are somewhere on the way between disquiet and uncertitude towards affirmation and faith, the triumphal "tragedy" of Thomas à Becket is what it was meant to be: a most faithful representation of the Christian witness on the earth. In the frozen moment of Thomas's martyrdom, a stasis is reached which resolves the contradiction between action and suffering, in the process making for an artist's triumph over time—creating a moment of artifice that will last as long as men have memories. In so doing, Eliot takes care of both the problem of evil and the issue of freedom of choice; for the year must renew itself. If we will let it.

But it is because no other playwright has made such extensive and intensive use of the Christ-image in modern theatre that Eliot's play finally centres so extraordinarily around the act of Thomas's martyrdom—removing it, ultimately, from the sphere of applicable critical terminology which we may have employed elsewhere as well. In the extended moment of Thomas's assassination, all the lines of the play converge—"rising" and "falling" actions leave their solid and dotted lines upon the graph; and a man ascends in the act of falling. The brute, beast, part of human nature, in effect, murders itself, leaving the spirit free to rise on its own afflatus. This is not a cozily contemporary view of body and soul, but it does appear to be Eliot's. Thomas's death is the unchosen effect of a chosen course of action, and represents the exercise of a freedom now denied his Church, Eliot would say: the freedom to accept the divine pattern without consulting human agencies, without deferring to human exigencies. More, it is a theatrical *tour-de-force*—the reduction to a single sustained instant of non-"action" of the entire drama we have been witnessing. Though one King Henry has condoned his death and another will destroy his tomb, Thomas dies triumphant in the shedding of blood which not only rebukes anti-disestablishmentarians of the present day, but also metaphorically defeats the enemy of human striving, time. His death is art.

NOTE

1   T.S. Eliot, *Murder in the Cathedral* (London, 1976). All page references appear parenthetically within my text.

7

O'Neill's Evangel of Peace: *The Iceman Cometh*

In the standard interpretations of the Biblical accounts of the ministry of Jesus, the ironic juxtaposition of his roles as Prince of Peace and Sword-Bringer is usually resolved by seeing Peace as the eternal goal of a lifetime of struggle. Thus the more unsettling implications of Jesus's doctrine—those which threaten the placidity of a comfortable, albeit unjustified, status-quo—can be viewed in terms of their final orientation to a pacific future existence. Thus does the Christian dispensation deal with the paradox so classically stated by Camus' Caligula (who handled matters rather differently): "Men die; and they are not happy."[1] To those who conclude that Christianity is death-centred, or who cannot participate in its most reassuring commitments, the existential predicament resulting from the clash of life- and death-values is apt to produce a caving-in from both sides, and a continuing state of death-in-life, or life-in-death. Small wonder that hardly a single significant dramatist, especially in recent times, has failed to envision theatrically a human existence that is tantamount to dreaming.

From Chekhov to Albee, the necessity of the subjective existence has repeatedly been posited and emphasised, and only the poet can dare to suggest, as Yeats does, the "answer" to Prufrock's overwhelming question:

> We perish into God and sink away
> Into reality—the rest's a dream.[2]

On the fast road from the notion best stated by Relling in Ibsen's *The Wild Duck*, that mankind cannot live without a "vital lie", to the contemporary commonplace that subjective reality is "real", or as good as real, the plays of Eugene O'Neill represent an important milestone. It is there that what we may call the Pirandellian alternative takes a crucial turn: that is, the idea of the "vital lie" becomes redefined from a non-truth that makes life possible to one which is alive by virtue of its discrepancy from objective "truth". *The Iceman Cometh* (1939)[3] is the clearest statement of O'Neill's own conclusions on this matter, conclusions which we find framed in structures borrowed from Christian myth. By means of a complicated interweaving of Christ-references, O'Neill promulgates a gospel of his own: that the truth kills, and that only death frees.

Eugene O'Neill is hardly the most subtle of playwrights, and the observations which I shall make in the course of my reading of the play will necessarily be premised on materials that have already been mined, however shallowly, before this. Moreover, it would be a critical commonplace to rely too heavily on the obvious fact that the play is rife with references to "God" and "Christ", almost always as expletives—though arguably just as often pertinently. I would claim, however, that *The Iceman Cometh* dramatizes the process by which a false or inadequate Messiah is succeeded by a better one—much the same process as involves Jim Casy and Tom Joad in John Steinbeck's classic novel *The Grapes of Wrath*. Failure to observe the operation of a kind of apostolic succession in both works can lead their readers, as it often has, to fundamental misunderstandings.

Though the play takes place in 1912 in Harry Hope's saloon, "a cheap ginmill of the five-cent whiskey, last-resort variety", and though the play is jammed with references to drinking and getting drunk, the end result of all this imbibing is to make possible the maintenance of "pipe dreams" as O'Neill repeatedly terms them; thus O'Neill uses a concrete addiction to support a metaphorical one. The setting (p. 571), with its singular black curtain dividing the world of the back room from the bar proper, is similarly conceived of in a way which combines elements of naturalistic and expressionistic stagecraft. (If the device seems Yeatsian, it ought to remind us of O'Neill's patent debt to Strindberg.) The black curtain

94

separates the outer and inner worlds, and with them the two "realities" known by the characters of the play. In its evident light-blocking capacity, it relates directly to the appearance-reality theme, or rather that of realities perceived or not perceived. And of course the eye-effect of O'Neill's contrived staging is to create, subliminally or ostensibly, a scene reminiscent of the Last Supper. This obvious observation is reinforced by the fact that we are indeed witnessing a "last" version of a ritual "feast", one with sacramental overtones, instituted by a Christ-figure to give one or another form of grace.

The play's overt interest in religious trappings extends to the three cardinal virtues; faith is explored rather fully, love too (implicitly), but most especially is the "virtue" (given the play's system of values) of hope, the mother of pipe dreams, considered. After all, we are in an establishment which—as such things go in modern drama—takes its very name and character from its owner, Harry Hope, and which caters to the needs of men who cannot cope with the world outside. All of its inmates, judging merely by the list of characters (p. 570), are individuals who exist, in reminiscence or intention, by means of selling illusions to others; the play's irony of character, given what is otherwise the familiar cross-section-of-society or ship-of-fools' collection of types, depends upon the interesting fact that what these persons are, or say they are, or say they were or someday hope to be, is in every instance a seller of illusions. We have the proprietor of a saloon, a circus man, a corrupt policeman, a would-be lawyer, a professional gambler, two soldiers, a war correspondent, two devotees of revolutionary causes, two bartenders, a self-deluding traitor, three whores, and a salesman. All sell others on images, or represent institutions riddled with falsehood. Con men, all of them, and with themselves as initial customers. O'Neill's character sketches, with which I shall not take the time to deal in detail, confirm this impression (pp. 574-77).

The very first speech in the play, made as a drink is being consumed, refers to "tomorrow", and calls upon the name of "Jees" (pp. 577-78). And Larry, to whom the speech is made by Rocky the bartender, wastes no time in developing the theme of tomorrows upon tomorrows (p. 578). Indeed, these opening lines make a religious interpretation of the play impossible to evade. For Larry almost immediately refers to "tomorrow", the day when all due bills are to be paid, as "the Feast of All Fools"; and he answers Rocky's mockery with a rejoinder that is appropriately parody-religious:

> LARRY: . . . Don't mock the faith! Have you no respect for religion, you unregenerate Wop? . . . To hell with the truth! As the history of the world proves, the truth has no bearing on anything . . . The lie of a pipe dream is what gives life to the whole misbegotten mad lot of us, drunk or sober . . .
>
> (p. 578)

Larry's use of one of O'Neill's favourite descriptive terms, "misbegotten" (he even uses it in the title of a later play), reminds us of one of his own black-Catholic religious suppositions: that we are born misbegotten—our being born itself an original sin—and unless we accept the pipe dream of a self-deceiving hope, we will remain "unregenerate", unreborn, unalive. It seems beyond doubt that Larry himself is the character who comes closest to resembling the author of the play, who was similarly bemused by mankind's need for illusion, had himself flirted with suicide at about the time the play takes place, and possessed both anarchist political leanings and the habit of phrasing mankind's dilemma in theological terminology. But I would prefer to leave that notion, like the identification of Strindberg with the Captain in *The Father*, for someone else to pursue: like the religious element in *Iceman*, it is a study capable of much mischief. For these reasons, I will not deal with every "fer Chris' sake", "Be God", and "Oh, Papa! Jesus!" that the play contains (pp. 579, 581).

More interesting are the implications of the presence of Hickey in Harry Hope's saloon. Both the title of the play and Rocky's reminder (p. 580) connect Hickman with the joke about his wife and the iceman; and the critical argument over whether the point of the title is to suggest the coming of death, which is clearly the case, or to remind us of an obscene joke, which it may, is to miss the point that both interpretations are correct and, furthermore, not mutually exclusive at all. If the iceman of the story is someone who cheats Hickey by having an adulterous liaison with Hickey's wife, then he stands in relation to Hickey, through her, as Hickey is towards the inmates of Harry Hope's: that is, he represents the destruction of illusions, the destroyer of the love affair, or marriage, between the individual and his dreams. More about this later, but for the moment it is interesting to note that Harry Hope is by reputation blind and deaf: that is, his awareness is selective, a trait appropriate to one running an establishment such as his. But to conclude the proportionality established above, if iceman is to Hickey as Hickey is to Hope's patrons, then Hickey cancels out of the system, being merely the agency by which Death comes to Harry Hope's, or death to hopes. If it is Larry who understands the resultant equation, then Hickey plays John the Baptist to Larry, whose gospel is unequivocally one of peace in death. And fittingly enough, it is Hickey who, as forerunner, is to die, while Larry is condemned to resurrection: that is, to "eternal" life.

At this point in the play, however, we are introduced to the character Parritt, who as his name most unsubtly suggests is a Judas-figure, a "stool-pigeon", yet whose function in the scheme I am outlining is as equivocal as Hickey's. For if Parritt is Judas, his betrayal is in the past, before the play begins; he does not appear to betray anyone in the play, unless by taking for himself the death craved by Larry. Interestingly, it is Larry who denies Parritt, Peter-like, on at least two occasions (pp. 583, 642) before sending him to his death. The first denial comes right after Rocky has described Parritt as someone who "don't belong", an expression which figures importantly in such other O'Neill plays as *The Hairy Ape*. As employed by O'Neill, the expression refers to one's role-awareness as an integral member of a human group, and is thus roughly equivalent to the illusory sense of personal worth; ironically, its opposite is a tragic separation from the community of human pipe dreamers: the self-reliance which, in a rejection of Emersonian values, is tantamount to death.

Joe's "parable" on the relationship of money to political theory (the word is Larry's) is followed by Parritt's first appearance, defensively denying that he possesses money which might be the reward for his betrayal of his mother and the Movement (pp. 584-85). But when Larry defines the nature of Harry Hope's for Parritt, describing the place as a "last harbour" beyond which no one can go but where "the appearances of life" are maintained by means of pipe dreams (of which he, Larry says, has none), Parritt gratefully responds to this expression of sympathy by saying, "Christ, Larry, I was glad to find you" (p. 587). Larry's ultimate function in the life of Parritt is to give him permission to kill himself; in terms of the play's development, Larry is thus able to perform for Parritt what Hickey is unable to do for the boys at Harry Hope's, but in the process, it can be argued, Larry gives his own "life", his singular commitment towards death. It is as bridge between the world of Harry Hope's and the outside realities represented by Parritt that Larry plays his role of "Old Foolosopher"—in effect, O'Neill's *raisonneur*.

"Yesterdays and tomorrows", that is where the men at Harry Hope's spend their mental excursions, Larry tells us (p. 587); the two are unified in the single cause which both Larry and Parritt have been affiliated with: the "Movement". As in Chekhov, the revolutionary alternative, with its logic or dialectics premised on historical necessity but justified by an ineluctable and glorious future, is being presented as perhaps the ultimate deception. "Mother", whom Parritt has betrayed, is more of an abstraction than a real presence, even of the offstage variety; readily identified with the Movement itself and with Faith, she is like the Holy Ghost completing the Trinity of Larry (hope betrayed) and Parritt (love betrayed)—to make use of at least one standard explanation of that mystery. Parritt tells us that Mother "feels about the Movement" the way a "revivalist preacher" feels "about religion. Anyone who loses faith in it is more than dead to her; he's a Judas who ought to be boiled in oil" (p. 589). But Larry has lost faith, and is by this definition such a "Judas" too. He rejects the notion that Mother may have ever forgiven him, referring to the Movement as "the One True Faith" (p. 589). It seems that Larry's loss of faith was due to his disillusionment with mankind in general, although he spent thirty years in fervent "devotion to the Cause" (p. 590). (Thirty years of apprenticeship prepared a Jesus for a Public Life.) And now, as is the implication of Larry's quotation from Heine, he has reached the conclusion that oblivion is best: that is, the state of never having been created (p. 591).

Larry informs Parritt, and ourselves, of the fact that the men at Harry Hope's are enormously contented: "It isn't often that men attain the true goal of their heart's desire" (p. 594). And in the same speech, we learn that Harry Hope's own wife has been dead for twenty years. Their women have vanished out of the lives of these men: Hickey, Harry, Parritt and, by extension, Larry. Small wonder that Willie Oban prays that "Hickey, the Great Salesman, will soon arrive bringing the blessed bourgeois long green!" (p. 596). "Would that Hickey or Death would come!" he continues. The contentment of men in the absence of their faithful spouses, or mothers, is noted by O'Neill: deprived of Faith, they can make do with Hope. We think necessarily of Arthur Miller's Salesman, with his parody of Hickey's situation, wanting to be the Great Salesman but having to live with Life's realities, yet swerved from dealing with them by an all-too-faithful wife, Linda. It is extremely unlikely that Miller did not use O'Neill's play as a source-text, nor that he wrote *Death of a Salesman* without wishing to extend its conception of the salesman as archetypal American dealer-in-dreams.

This is perhaps the appropriate point at which to begin a discussion of O'Neill's manipulation of sexual imagery in *Iceman*. Certainly he, like Ibsen and Shaw before him, found it useful to take advantage of audience assumptions about proper sex roles, and attributes, for men and women. And like his predecessors, he could play upon those assumptions in order to extend, repudiate, or simply challenge them; the offstage women in this play, then, can be said to represent its philosophical variables—the elements which male intellectuality cannot quite get under control. Parritt, for instance, is both attracted to and repulsed by whores (pp. 591, 594, 615), perhaps because his own mother possessed the positive and negative qualities of that "sort" of woman in measures impossible to evaluate. Harry Hope's late wife was an adoring nag (p. 603), and his recollections of her parallel those of the widower in Pinter's *The Homecoming*. And in the midst of whorish anecdotes about their trade, Hickey is introduced— both as an encountered offstage presence, and then as an onstage one. Each time, it is as someone coming to "save" the multitude from their failings (pp. 617-18). It is their pipe dreams Hickey would save them from, and he tells them that he is the son of a preacher (pp. 621-22) (again, the inherited preoccupations of a pioneer father are a significant part of

99

Arthur Miller's *Salesman*'s sample case). And as though he had recreated the universe, or had taken his own advice, the messenger of peace sinks into the temporary oblivion of exhausted sleep (p. 625), bringing the first act to a close. Hickey's deathly sleep is a visual prediction of the release of death which his doctrine promises.

In Act II, the deathly black curtain is in place throughout, but the back room is prepared for a "festivity". The birthday cake, with its six candles, might evoke memories of Christmas, but the presence of the black curtain, the ominous feeling that quickly develops, and the catafalque-number of candles probably remind us of impending death—Good Friday without a succeeding Easter, although rebirth and resurrection are Hickey's themes (pp. 628-29). Perhaps we also remember Larry's image for Harry Hope's earlier on: that of a "grave-yard" (p. 587). Certainly spiritual regeneration is in the air; even the streetwalker Pearl refers to giving up one's pipe dream as a conversion (p. 633). Yet the application of these terms is hedged about with irony; O'Neill's people are apt to make the common error of imputing their own psychological disorders onto others, projecting their own states of mind onto their neighbours. So that when Hickey arrives and calls Larry "Old Cemetery, the Barker for the Big Sleep" (p. 639), we might consider the degree to which he is himself the salesman of death, for he chooses a metaphor of huckstering. Yet Hickey is able to diagnose Larry's condition as a waiting for death that masks a real fear of death, and a clinging to life; what *he* offers, Hickey continues, is "real peace", which he defines as not caring about either life or death (p. 641). Thus Hickey's gospel is not one of Christian activism, but rather an Oriental indifference that is beyond all hope. But the practical effect of this philosophy is, of course, to lead to death directly—a course, he hints to Larry, that would make an appropriate direction to give to Parritt (p. 642).

In speaking of Parritt, Hickey makes an interesting reference to "real love" as the "stuff that crucifies you" (p. 642). What follows is a page of speculation by Hickey and Larry about love, women, and the Movement; the upshot would seem to be a confirmation of the proportionality spoken of earlier, with the addition of a new element: the conception of love (the

100

Movement, Parritt's mother, Parritt's woman, as deeply related to) as a sacrificial cross which one can accept or reject. A further implication may be said to be that Parritt, who eventually accepts the burden of his personal cross, and with it his death, is also a bit of a Christ-figure, though it is far more common to note the manner of his death, and to compare it with Judas's. But I think it useful to note the degree to which O'Neill establishes the parallelism among not only Hickey and Parritt—which we find dramatically supported by juxtaposed speeches later in the play—but Larry and perhaps Harry Hope as well, all of them "burdened" by the cross of a love-hate relationship with a believing woman. In Larry's case, a discussion with Parritt (pp. 646-47) reveals that Parritt's mother's faith in Larry may have been so oppressive that he made use of her promiscuity and his loss of faith in the Movement as reasons for rejecting the demands of her love. If Parritt's understanding of Larry is correct, then the relationship between them becomes even more interesting, for both of them have betrayed the same woman, both of them have found there to be "something not human" about Hickey (p. 648), and each of them understands the other implicitly. Acceptance of this view leads to the possible conclusion that in giving Parritt permission to die, Larry may be relieving himself of still another burdensome demand on his consience, and in the process denying Parritt for the third time. But all such events, in this play, are fraught with ambiguity, for the goals of our illusions (Hickey says, speaking of Larry's desire for death; p. 657) are meaningful only as long as we keep ourselves from attaining them.

These goals are based on false projections of our needs, Hickey says, and the falsity is premised on our senses of guilt, the "remorse that nags at you and makes you hide behind lousy pipe dreams about tomorrow" (p. 661). Even Hickey, who describes himself as a "cheater", has invented the story about the iceman to keep his obligations to Evelyn at bay, and now she has achieved "peace" in death (Hickey reveals, closing the second act; p. 663). But the revelation brings only unease; what is said masks what remains unsaid, and this feast of cake and wine and candles takes on an ominous sort of truth-telling, group-therapy sensation of discomfort. We are in for more upsetting disclosures, for Larry has already called the evening "a second feast of Belshazzar, with Hickey to do the writing on the wall!" (p. 644). Larry's suggestion takes Hickey, at least for the moment, out of the category of Christ-figures, and allies him instead with those Old Testament prophets to whom the people will not listen (as in Arden and Shaw), or with the owner of the spiritual hand which writes a promise of destruction on the wall of Babylon in Daniel 5. With such understanding, death comes; and we remember, too, Hugo's refrain (based on Psalm 137) about languishing in Babylon: of which more later.

As Act III begins, the stage set is illuminated with daylight— presumably the light brought by Hickey, in effect—but it does not penetrate as far as the back room, as the stage directions make clear (p. 664). Hickey's light may be ambiguous, there- fore, but it is enough to make Parritt begin to think that his mother is dead, and that Larry might have been his father—or so he once thought (pp. 666-67). Larry's angry denial of this all-too-real and interesting possibility, given the play's Freudian preoccupations and its discussions of guilt, is what might also be credited as his third denial of Parritt. Certain enough is the way that Hickey's revelation that Evelyn is dead has affected Parritt, the association of one woman with another allowing his confession to flow forth—starting with the ugly fact — if it is a fact — that he did it all for money (p. 667). Thereafter Parritt begins to make reference to Mother whenever a particularly penetrating revelation about Evelyn is made; for instance, Rocky and Larry's speculation on whether Evelyn might have committed suicide over Hickey's infidelity moves Parritt to cite the tenacity with which Mother clings to life (p. 668). Larry almost immediately refuses to "judge" Parritt when the latter asks if he is expected to take Larry's place in leaping off the fire-escape; yet this seemingly Christlike refusal on Larry's part is actually no such thing, but a simple rejection of involvement in Parritt's life, a denial of responsibility which may, as the play has suggested, be actually parental.

Several pages, or minutes of performance time, are now given over to a survey of the effects of Hickey's urgings on the denizens of Harry Hope's. At its conclusion, Parritt resumes the discussion of his motivations: first accusing Larry of still loving the Movement, he changes to an accusation that Larry still

loves Mother—while Mother loves only the Movement. It is
Larry's acquiescence in his denial of hatred for his mother that
Parritt asks, but Larry turns him down: "For the love of Christ,
will you leave me in peace! I've told you you can't make me
judge you! . . . To hell with you." but Larry's refusal to judge
(lest he be judged?), while inducing despair in Parritt, leads
Larry to drink—and to the sudden insight that Death is "the
Iceman Hickey called to his home" (p. 680). Again the other
characters take their turns, this time being thrust out into the
world by Hickey, in order that they have a chance to recognize
their illusions as precisely that. Now it's Larry's turn, but the
Old Foolosopher is capable of articulating exactly what his
self-deception is even as he denies its control over him:

> LARRY: . . . I'm afraid to live, am I?—and even more afraid to
> die! So I sit here, with my pride drowned on the bottom of a
> bottle, keeping drunk so I won't see myself shaking in my
> britches with fright, or hear myself whining and praying:
> Beloved Christ, let me live a little longer at any price! If it's only
> for a few days more, or a few hours even, have mercy, Almighty
> God, and let me still clutch greedily to my yellow heart this sweet
> treasure, this jewel beyond price, the dirty, stinking bit of
> withered old flesh which is my beautiful little life!
>
> (p. 689)

It is the self which is the source of fears, like the "ghost
automobile" which almost runs Harry down—or does, for he
admits that something did run over him: "Must have been
myself, I guess" (p. 691).

Yet Larry demurs; bitterly attacking Hickey's gift as "the
peace of death" (p. 692), he succeeds in getting Hickey to reveal
that his wife has been murdered. The awful truth begins to
dawn on Larry, and the motivation for Hickey's murder of
Evelyn is telegraphed ahead by Hope's and Parritt's identification of women in their lives with Evelyn (pp. 693-95). Hugo
loses control, though no one pays attention to him, and in the
process reveals himself as something other than what he
pretends to be: an elitist instead of a proletarian sympathizer;
he also helps end the act on a chilling note, speaking of life as "a

crazy monkey-face" and the illusion of contentment as leading to the discovery, "Always there is blood beneath the willow trees!" (p. 695). Evelyn, a name derived from Eve, is in its very meaning equivalent to "life", so that what Hickey is about to admit to having done is tantamount to murdering life itself—and in his own case, equivalent to it. Yet this is the only release from the penalty of living, and Larry is beginning to embrace death with a sort of Robinson Jeffers stoicism that is, eventually, a complicity in what Hickey has accomplished.

In the fourth act, "oppressive stagnation" has set in, and the characters have become mechanical, waxlike (p. 696). Parritt accuses Larry of coveting a death off the fire-escape, another instance of an individual's charging others with his own proclivities (pp. 700-1). Parritt's effort is intended to get some sympathetic response from Larry, even if only a warrant for his own self-execution. But Larry is more concerned with the implications of Hickey's mission of "peace", and he notes with "sardonic pity" the effects of that peace on Rocky; the latter offers to take in first Parritt, then Larry himself, as an apprentice manager of prostitutes, but Larry criticizes Hickey's peace as not "contented enough, if you have to make everyone else a pimp, too" (p. 702). Thus one alternative to the stark confrontation with the truth of one's existence is rejected by Larry, and implicitly by O'Neill as well.

When Hickey finally confesses to having killed Evelyn (p. 706), Parritt reminds Larry what he already knows, or will soon: that "It's worse if you kill someone and they have to go on living" (p. 706). Life and death are being equated here, and most peculiarly; the equation is augmented by the arrival of the detectives Moran and Lieb, their names—as is often noted—suggestive of death and life. They are a team, and they come for you together (p. 708). And now the ongoing confession of both Hickey and Parritt continues, the two admissions made curiously parallel by the same self-deceptions, at least initially—that both men had loved the women they "killed" (killed to death, that is, as well as killed to continued life, as Parritt has put it) (p. 709). The irony of Hickey's story is that it maintains a false image of his motivations, for it keeps up the lie of his love for his wife, and by that means sustains her faith in him—the very thing he says he set out to destroy. He was the great salesman who prospered by taking advantage of others' pipe dreams, he admits; yet he has just finished saying that Evelyn's love and faith made him believe her proclamations of his essential integrity and the genuineness of his intentions to reform. Thus the seller of dreams was himself their victim—a situational irony which must have had great appeal to Arthur Miller, who examined the same problem in greater depth in *Death of a Salesman*. For O'Neill, however, the representative Americanness of his character is less important than the simple pathos of their human predicaments—especially as expressed in sexual bewilderment. Hickey—like Willy Loman—wanted a woman he could relax with, be relieved of a false self-image with, and thus enjoy the absence of shame with (pp. 711-12).

Adultery provided that relief, an hiatus from the rigours of role-playing as much as from the strictures of the marriage contract, its moral demands. Cora, who knows this game from the other side, interjects a line about constantly having to pretend a joke was funny, revealing that Hickey's condition is epidemic in proportions (p. 712). And as surely as in Ibsen, it leads to disease, thematically the metaphor for moral contagion, or sickness of the soul. Hence all the references to adultery in *Iceman*, beginning with its title: the paramount interpersonal and intersexual form of fooling another party, it represents the ultimate transgression of the positive role of woman, and with it the whole male-female relationship. This is why the Hope establishment is also the headquarters of a brothel system—and why so many weights of love betrayed become, inevitably, so many hates.

Thus Hickey had even, ostensibly jokingly, suggested that his wife take a lover, and later invented the iceman story. And thus he needed to tear up her picture after her murder—because, he says, he "didn't need it any more", but obviously because it reminded him of the guilt she caused him to feel. For the same reasons, Parritt burned his mother's picture, although his reasons are even more interesting—and thematically relevant. It was because her "eyes followed [him] all the time", seemingly wanting him dead. (One recalls portraits of Christ which bear eyes that supposedly follow the onlooker around the room.) And so love turned to hate, first for the "pipe dream" offered by the other party, then for the party herself. Of course, these hatreds of offstage parties are the mask for hatreds of the self (pp. 713-14). Therefore, even as the others listen as though for the last breath of a dying man (p. 714), Hickey reaches the point of admitting his killing—so that Evelyn might "never wake up from her dream" (p. 715). The admission comes even though Harry Hope has tried to forestall it by saying, "Give us a rest, for the love of Christ!" (p. 715). And just as suddenly, Parritt takes the process an unwanted step further, confessing hatred for Mother—a step which Hickey almost immediately follows in (p. 716).

But that is going too far: Hickey never meant to say that much, never knew he knew it at all. He quickly decides he was "insane" to have spoken his hatred, yet makes it clear he does not want exemption from the Chair for his insanity (pp. 716-18). For his hopes and pipe dreams are gone now, but he would never have said he hated the only woman he had ever loved—or at least that is what he claims. Hickey is taken away, and now it is Parritt's turn. The young man adds a new note to what Hickey has been saying, for while Hickey's murder resulted in apparent release for the murderer, in death, there will be no such pat solution for Parritt—unless Larry intervenes. And while Hickey's motivation is revealed as hatred, the phrase with which he speaks of it to Evelyn is repeated by Parritt, almost word for word—but with a significant addition. "You know what you can do with your freedom pipe dream now, don't you, you damned old bitch!", he says he thought afterwards; he does not claim to have been crazy, but he does add the reference to freedom. Now freedom is the element represented by Mother but not by Evelyn, for the wife—life—is a bond, but maternity is possibility, futurity; and therefore Parritt brings to the play a rejection of another sort of "pipe dream": the chance of choosing actions freely, and having them make a difference. O'Neill's use of literal and metaphorical murder in order to deny existential freedom makes for fascinating comparisons with the suggestions of Sartre and Camus—just as his use of the brothel as the place where roles are played out anticipates the theatrical conceptions of Jean Genet. Whatever the possibility of comparison, Parritt's revelations enrage Larry, who orders Parritt to die. And Parritt, the bird which not only talks but also repeats what it is told, is only too glad for the chance to echo

Hickey in act as well as word (pp. 719-20). And the deaths of Harry Hope's wife in the past, and Hickey's in the present, create a pattern that is completed by Mother's "death" in Parritt, in whom she is reflected.

And if Harry Hope's eventual rejection of his dead wife Bessie is reminiscent of Harold Pinter's Max's way of talking about *his* dead wife Jessie in *The Homecoming*, it is even more pertinent to compare Moran and Lieb, as agents of retribution for guilt, to the Goldberg and McCann of Pinter's *The Birthday Party*. For Pinter has retained O'Neill's notion of complicity in one's own punishment, but deliberately obscured the nature of the guilt—which is likely similar in type to Parritt's. For when Parritt responds to Larry's orders with gratitude, Larry begins to "plead": "Go, for the love of Christ, you mad tortured bastard, for your own sake!" (p. 720). At this, the misbegotten Parritt stammers an emotional, "Jesus, Larry, thanks" (p. 721). Thus Hickey's function as false Messiah is taken over, redeemed and transformed, by Larry, who brings Parritt the only true peace, the peace of death. Ironically, Hickey is now identified by Hugo as a seller of death, as in a sandman's sort of way he is—by influence; but Parritt is off, by Larry's leave, to the land of tomorrow, where he will buy Hugo a drink "beneath the willow trees" (p. 721). In this world, as Harry told Hugo earlier, "There ain't any cool willow trees—except you grow your own in a bottle" (p. 691). With Hickey—and Parritt, soon—gone, the drinks begin to have their old kick again, and the pipe dreams are revived—except for Larry, who awaits Parritt's death by calling on Christ (p. 722). Similarly, perhaps, the whores cry a relieved "Jees!" when they hear what has happened to Hickey (p. 725).

And one "Jees" more—Rocky uses the word in noting that Larry is over in the corner (still waiting for the sound of Parritt's falling body), apparently with his eyes shut; what Rocky might instinctively, but not intellectually, recognise in the pose is a kind of Gethsemane, with Larry "torturedly arguing to himself":

> LARRY: . . . It's the only way out for him! For the peace of all concerned, as Hickey said! . . . God damn his yellow soul, if he doesn't soon, I'll go up and throw him off . . .
>
> (p. 726)

But his suffering is short-lived; he is rescued from it by the awful
sound of Parritt's body falling, though none of the others
recognises it for what it is (the dramatic effect is like the suicide
at the end of *The Seagull* in this respect). And now Larry relaxes,
like Alison at the end of *Look Back in Anger:*

> LARRY: . . . Poor devil! *(A long-forgotten faith returns to him for a
> moment and he mumbles)* God rest his soul in peace. *(He opens his
> eyes—with a bitter self-derision)* Ah, the damned pity—the wrong
> kind, as Hickey said! Be God, there's no hope! I'll never be a
> success in the grandstand—or anywhere else! Life is too much for
> me! I'll be a weak fool looking with pity at the two sides of
> everything till the day I die! *(With an intense bitter sincerity)* May
> that day come soon! *(He pauses startledly, surprised at himself—then
> with a sardonic grin)* Be God, I'm the only real convert to death
> Hickey made here. From the bottom of my coward's heart I
> mean that now!

(pp. 726-27)

Realising that Hickey has indeed influenced him releases Larry
for death, and grants him peace—the peace of the dead-in-life.
Similarly, his "conversion", a rebirth of the spirit—however
ironically it occurs—confirms the Christhood of Hickey. Yet the
sacrificial figure, at the end, has been Parritt, who even parrots,
or parodies, Hickey's "sacrifice". Indeed, as in the aforementioned *Look Back in Anger* or *The Wild Duck* or *Who's Afraid of
Virginia Woolf?*, the death of the child, the "death" of the
"child", accomplishes the reuniting of the parents. In this case,
it is the "child", perhaps literally so, of Larry and Mother,
Larry and freedom. And with its death, hope dies too.

Clearly the Christhood is diffused in *The Iceman Cometh*, even
extending to the supposed Judas-figure (he *is* that, but it will be
noted that Parritt betrays nothing of what Hickey comes to
deliver, but parallels his efforts at every turn). Just as clearly,
Hickey is a sort of false Messiah, if not an Antichrist, at least to
us, if not to O'Neill. For he promises peace, as Jesus in fact did
not. And what he brings to Larry, if that can be said to be the
process which is carried out, is the quasi-zombie status of those
resigned to death. At this point, it seems appropriate to quote
the entire 137th psalm (from the Gideon edition of which I have
removed the italics):

108

BY the rivers of Babylon, there we sat down, yea, we wept, when we remembered Zion.

2 We hanged our harps upon the willows in the midst thereof.

3 For there they that carried us away captive required of us a song; and they that wasted us required of us mirth, saying, Sing us one of the songs of Zion.

4 How shall we sing the LORD's song in a strange land?

5 If I forget thee, O Jerusalem, let my right hand forget her cunning.

6 If I do not remember thee, let my tongue cleave to the roof of my mouth; if I prefer not Jerusalem to my chief joy.

7 Remember, O LORD, the children of Edom in the day of Jerusalem; who said, Rase it, rase it, even to the foundation thereof.

8 O daughter of Babylon, who art to be destroyed; happy shall he be, that rewardeth thee as thou hast served us.

9 Happy shall he be, that taketh and dasheth thy little ones against the stones.

Though as I write this this psalm has provided the lyrics for a hit song in England and much of North America, it is quite clearly a nasty little ditty once it gets going. It is then like Hugo's *Carmagnole*, which persists, as a dance of death, when all the other party songs have ended.

It is cool beneath the willow trees, because we have plenty to drink. Though they make us sing, our songs make us nostalgic for our home (Desdemona, about to die, sang of willow). We are married to false gods; adulteries dissuade us from progeny. Nevertheless, we languish here, unable to move. Let us therefore sing.

I think of another song, and wonder if O'Neill had it in mind:

> There is a tavern in the town,
> And there my true love sits him down,
> And drinks his wine with laughter and with glee,
> And never, never thinks of me.
>
> Adieu, adieu, kind friends, adieu, adieu, adieu,
> I can no longer stay with you.
> I'll hang my harp on a weeping willow-tree,
> And may the world go well with thee.[4]

It has all the elements encountered in *Iceman*: false love, sorrow

109

and hopeless living, life-in-death, and song and drink as a distraction. It is also the play's setting, and its action. (There is the Christ who died for us, and the Christ who turned the water into wine.) It is the death of children, the end of self-assertion, and the execution of our freedom. It is the pathos of our hope. Perhaps that is because the play mirrors the state of mind of its creator, of whom Tennessee Williams is quoted as saying, with regard to their correspondence about *Iceman*, that he "gave birth to the American theatre and died for it."[5]

NOTES

1 Albert Camus, *Caligula and Three Other Plays* (New York, 1966), p.8.
2 William Butler Yeats, *The Hour-Glass*, in *The Collected Plays of W.B. Yeats* (New York, 1963), p. 210.
3 Eugene O'Neill, *The Iceman Cometh* in *The Plays of Eugene O'Neill*, 3 (New York, 1954). All page references appear parenthetically within my text.
4 "Anonymous", in *Bartlett's Familiar Quotations* (Boston, 1968), p. 1100.
5 Arthur and Barbara Gelb, *O'Neill* (New York, 1973), p. 877.

8

Osborne's Gospel of Commitment: *Look Back in Anger*

Twenty years in not a long time for an "angry" play to hold its heat, nor is it too short a span to protect such a play from "dating". Yet if the social sources of *Look Back in Anger*[1] seem rooted in the distant past, the eloquence of its tirades is as marked as ever, and is likely to remain so. However unadventurous its Ibsenian structure and plotting, John Osborne's play still captivates—perhaps because we are finally as uncertain as we were twenty years ago as to what *Look Back in Anger* "says".

I intend to present a reading of the play premised on the notion of Jimmy Porter as existential hero-in-the-making, a secular Christ who appears to stand at the play's end having all he needs to become the sort of social saviour Osborne seems to think his country badly needs—creating in the process a palpable "improvement" in the Biblical Christ, who as the hostage of churches is therefore woefully deficient. This argument does not rest on Jimmy's possession of that magical first initial, nor on his surname's suggestion of—among other things—the role of burden-carrier; moreover, we are not required to consider Biblical allusions beyond those aspects of the life of Christ that would be familiar to a literate audience. Yet Osborne's hero may be considered as deliberately Messianic in character: as someone destined to preserve the best of Englishness by playing a redemptive part in the reshaping of his country.

Though Osborne does not appear to know exactly *how* his

hero may accomplish this enormous, Arthurian task, his ending is neither despairing, on the one hand, nor vaguely and sentimentally romantic on the other. Jimmy and Alison, back together again, are the complete ingredients for a better tomorrow, the play seems to be saying. Whether they bring one about or not remains very much to be seen.

A reading of the play's five scenes will demonstrate the interworking of its dramatic elements—both the obvious and the less apparent—once those elements are clearly identified. In its opening stage directions, the play provides both the joint motifs of animal counterparts for Jimmy and Alison— respectively, bear and squirrel—and the "zoo" or "jungle" milieu for them to perform in (p. 9); the audience cannot miss noting the presence of these stuffed animals, which the actors refer to and even employ as surrogate selves. The bear, we notice in the text, is "tattered", while the squirrel is "soft, woolly". Squirrel and bear are therefore precisely what Alison and Jimmy are described as, yet also represent toy creatures capable of communicating only within a children's literature or cartoon world. Indeed, the atmosphere is said to be "all cloud and shadows" (p. 10): some definition is patently overdue.

Cliff is described as "relaxed"—an adjective which is not applied to Alison until the ending of the play. As the male "natural counterpoint" of Jimmy (p. 10), Cliff is destined to be replaced by a female figure who also embodies a requisite sexuality. By this process, the rough bear is presumably gentled, while the soft squirrel is tested by adversity. In formulaic expression, the play is simplistically catalytic: $(J+A+C) +H$ becomes $(J+H+C) -A$ becomes $(J+H) -C$, which with the return of a "new" Alison, A_2, becomes $(J+A_2) -H$. Particles dislodge particles, yet Jimmy remains the nucleus of each relationship.

So much has been noted before, but less obvious is the context of sacrifice in which all of these changes occur. The second Alison is now also "tattered" by loss, like Jimmy; and the loss has been her "first" (p. 92). Ironically, that loss is triggered by a gain, a gift: it is Jimmy's child (and all their future children) that she loses (that they lose), and Jimmy prophesies, even calls for, such a loss—like the Old Testament God of Abraham. It is as if the play makes the obvious point

112

that squirrels and bears cannot breed in the normal way; the posterity of Jimmy and Alison must therefore be spiritual if it is to exist at all. And finally, we must note that Jimmy Porter preaches a gospel of sacrifice meant primarily for other people: a kind of spiritual/physical pinching yourself to see if you're awake; a wounding to see if you're alive. Himself having already gone through such a pain (directly as well as emphatically), he can define living as, essentially, the consciousness of loss.

One thinks, perhaps, of the trapped fox of legend, rather than of squirrels and bears—the creature which gnaws away a limb to free its body. Yet Osborne makes it clear that Jimmy desires more than simply to exist; he wants to *do*, to *act*. It is thus that the parody-Christness of Jimmy operates. Like Brecht and other writers who reject an institutional Christianity, John Osborne presents a system that is, in essence, the improved version of what it would throw away. Out with the genteel Christ of the tame establishment Church, and in with the figure who cleansed the temple of moneychangers—the passionate spokesman for social change.

One must remember Jimmy's ironic occupation, the role he has donned like homespun: seller of sweets from a market stall. Like the addition to sweet things characteristic of the persons in John Steinbeck's *The Wayward Bus*, the craving of Osborne's society is for that which has been sugar-coated, glamourized, obscured. It is rather like the girl whose letter appears in the newspaper Jimmy is reading: she wants to give in to her boy friend, but also keep her "respect"; Jimmy calls her a "stupid bitch" (p. 13). As for himself, he is capable of sublimation, if substituting food for sex is exactly that. "Oh, yes, yes, yes. I like to eat. I'd like to live too," he tells Cliff—as if living were an ambition for the future (p. 12).

All these appetites (dulled on "sweets"?): like the Bishop of Bromley Jimmy claims to be reading about, it is a world of Christians refusing to worry about the poor, and instead dutifully manufacturing H-Bombs (pp. 13-14). In a further example, a woman gets mauled at an evangelical rally by enthusiastic "Christian Soldiers" (p. 14). No wonder Jimmy finds Sundays meaningless—a faithless ritual of "reading the papers, drinking tea, ironing", by means of which one's life is wasted away (pp. 14-15). What he wants is "enthusiasm", a

113

fact he recognises in his parody-cry of "Hallelujah! I'm alive!" and in his proposal that all of them "pretend" to be living human beings (p. 15).

Alison, says Jimmy, is so indifferent (a crime that Jesus spoke out against violently) that she would even get used to paradise after five minutes there (p. 16). In her company, he spends Sundays of dulling calm and deceptive "peace":

> Nobody thinks, nobody cares. No beliefs, no convictions and no enthusiasm. Just another Sunday evening.
>
> (p. 17)

A cultural Tory, Jimmy listens to the music of Vaughan Williams—post-Elgarian music to be sure, but arguably the expression of a musical establishment. Longing for the days of Empire even though he knows his impression of a prouder England is largely false and even though the contradiction with his principles is obvious, he notes that "it's pretty dreary living in the American age" (p. 17).

Jimmy's past had had its moments, of course—such as with his mistress Madeline (of all names!), an older woman with whom "the delight of being awake, and watching" was a constant, epic "adventure" (pp. 18-19). But now he lives with Alison, the very thought of whose family (those present-day relics of Empire) makes him fantasize himself as a Roman, "Sextus", who loses his wife, "Lady Pusillanimous", to "those beefcake Christians" (p. 22)—an interesting inversion of Swinburnian notions. It is such a capturing that that Christian Helena (is she named for the finder of the True Cross?) will shortly perform on him.

Jimmy would seem to be blaming women generally for having brought us all to this pass; his misogyny expresses itself in a tirade that culminates in his bewailing "the eternal flaming racket of the female"—whereupon the church bells begin to ring outside, as if on cue (p. 25). We should not ignore the references to "flaming", "hell", "God", etc., in this play any more than in reading Edward Albee's *The Zoo Story*, but one hardly needs them to establish the fact of Jimmy's connection of femaleness with the Church—and masculinity, by extension, with "life", "enthusiasm", and the rest of his list of virtues. There is no gainsaying the sexist residue in Jimmy's character,

114

even after love has burned away the grosser excesses of his rage.

And burning is what Jimmy literally does to Alison a moment later, when his roughhousing with Cliff causes the hot iron to fall against her arm (p. 26); he later admits that the act had been deliberate (p. 33). Yet Alison's rejection of love's demands is a parallel cruelty (p. 27); she admits to Cliff when Jimmy is out of the room that she had "pretended not to be listening" when he had poured out his heart to her (p. 28). This deliberate coldness made Jimmy "savage", of course; and Cliff calls the process of mutual hurting "tearing the insides out of each other" (p. 28). Just as strategically as in the earlier use of the church bells for emphasis, Osborne follows this remark with the revelation of Alison's pregnancy, of which Jimmy is still ignorant; she cannot tell him yet for fear he might think it a device for gaining control over him.

The references in this play to love as "fire", and as a matter of guts and devouring—and the assumption that life is based on such loving—are reminiscent of the mystical devotional poetry of an earlier age. Jimmy's "private morality", says Alison, is "pretty free" but "very harsh too" (p. 30); so that when Cliff calls Jimmy "just an old Puritan at heart" (p. 31), he is not wide of the mark. The Lawrentian scene of Jimmy and Cliff's game of bear and mouse yields to a love-game of bear and squirrel (pp. 32-4) that is almost embarrassingly intimate; but the shocking revelation that Jimmy and Alison do in fact love one another desperately, which might have led to Alison's revelation of her pregnancy, is deflected by the Ibsen-timely phone call from Helena, one of Jimmy's "natural enemies" (p. 35).

Jealous of Alison, Jimmy has become "predatory" (p. 36); as Helena approaches, the imagery of animal existence becomes overwhelming. Incredibly, Jimmy tells Alison "If you could have a child, and it would die [then you might] become a recognisable human being." He describes her passion in lovemaking as that of a "python. She just devours me whole every time, as if I were some over-large rabbit"; then he points to "that bulge around her navel" as his devoured self, still not realising that it is in fact "him" there (p. 37). He exits, ending Act I, after saying that he is "buried alive down there, and going mad" (p. 38), as if reflecting Osborne's chillingly intellectualised uses of pregnancy in this play.

Act II is a marking of time, but also a clarification of issues and backgrounds. Helena is called "the gracious representative of visiting royalty"—"middle-class womanhood" (p. 39). She finds Jimmy's antagonism "horrifying . . . and oddly exciting" (p. 41), yet clucks over the *ménage à trois* she has joined. After further expository matter, Alison describes the way Jimmy first impressed her:

> It had been such a lovely day, and he'd been in the sun. Everything about him seemed to burn, his face, the edges of his hair glistened and seemed to spring off his head, and his eyes were so blue and full of the sun.
>
> (p. 45)

She continues this extraordinary description by remembering him going "into battle with his axe swinging round his head—frail, and so full of fire." She has fallen in love with the Jimmy she has helped turn into a remnant of himself; with her, they were "poor silly little animals", "all love, and no brains" and "full of dumb, uncomplicated affection for each other", but now are—in Helena's phrase—a "menagerie" (p. 47). Her vision of a Christ-Apollo has become the denizen of a domestic zoo.

Jimmy thinks that the pull of family and friends is what keeps Alison from becoming a living being; he baits Helena by referring to Alison's friends as "chocolate meringues"—"Sweet and sticky on the outside . . . inside, all white, messy and disgusting" (p. 49). This expressionistic inversion of Christ's whited-sepulchre image is Jimmy's attack on a sexuality laden with false spirituality. And when Helena announces that she is taking Alison to church with her, the latter mocks Jimmy in just the same sort of language of the godlike she has recently used for praising him. Jimmy is driven to peaks of invective, assaulting on behalf of his lost "chivalry" not only Alison's mother ("She's as rough as a night in a Bombay brothel, and as tough as a matelot's arm.") but also Alison herself. Yet if Alison's mother calls forth Jimmy's most splendidly articulate insults, her daughter elicits only fatigue: her weight on "that poor old charger of mine"—"the old grey mare that actually once led the charge against the old order"—was "too much for her. She just dropped dead on the way" (pp. 51–2). This is surely self-pity, but the question is one of degree of justification.

Helena's cool respectability ("genuflecting sin jobber" as Jimmy calls her [p. 53]) is winning the day. Jimmy strikes out in panic, predicting the bodily corruption of Alison's mother in excessive terms and promising to write a book about "us all" that will be "recollected in fire, and blood. My blood" (p. 54). When Helena ignores the martyrdom Jimmy is describing in order to protest that his response to Alison's merely going to church is excessive, Jimmy wonders whether she even understands him. But Alison does: "Oh, don't try and take his suffering away from him—he'd be lost without it" (p. 54). What Alison sees that Helena may not is that Jimmy has made himself Christ of his own substitute religion, and that his wife's betrayal is therefore apostasy.

Jimmy means it: he calls Helena "this saint in Dior's clothing"—she is by profession an actress, a pretender—and not only a "cow" but "a sacred cow as well!" He describes her to Cliff as "an expert in the New Economics . . . of the Supernatural. It's all a simple matter of payments and penalties." Maintaining this economic imagery throughout, and applying the notion of capitalist exploitation to spiritual affairs, he assaults the religious revival and its "apocalyptic share pushers" who are betraying "Reason and Progress" and "free inquiry". "Tell me, what could be more gilt-edged than the next world! It's a capital gain, and it's all yours." Then he shifts to outlandish sanitary-engineering imagery to describe Helena, who in her "romantic" hearkening back to the "light" of the Dark Ages is like someone who prefers living in "a lovely little cottage of the soul": away from twentieth-century reality and "all the conveniences we've fought to get for centuries", she would rather "go down to the ecstatic little shed at the bottom of the garden to relieve her sense of guilt" (pp. 55-6). If the handling of the social theme is Ibsenian, the obsessions are Luther's. Helena is unmoved.

Jimmy's view of life inextricably connects corruption, sex, and death. He and Helena court one another with insults, among which sources of ultimately sexual excitement is the claim that Helena's never having seen someone die constitutes "a pretty bad case of virginity" (p. 58). He then offers a heartfelt memory of his own father's death by way of corrective: he remembers the dying man's "sweet, sickly smell", his commitment to causes, such as the Spanish Civil War, that his mother would not share in, and how his dying made Jimmy an expert in "love . . . betrayal . . . and death" by the age of ten (p. 58). These are, of course, the elements of life for Jimmy, the inverted values of a self-made Christ—one inescapably human, and divine only in spirit.

A last appeal to Alison: he asks if she will desert him without caring what people "do" to him (the question of Jesus in the Garden), then abruptly flies into another rage, calling her "Judas"—at which Alison, "blood" having been drawn at last, hurls to the floor the cup she has been holding. Is this, in effect, mock-sacrilege? It is at least ironic that all Alison wants is "a little peace". "Peace! God! She wants peace!" Jimmy gasps; in his eyes, Alison's "peace" is death: it is killing him. But this Christ, if he is one, brings not peace but a sword. Like Jerry in *The Zoo Story* again, he uses primarily verbal violence to get through desensitised skins (pp. 58-9). With Jimmy offstage, Cliff says that their household has usually always been "a very narrow strip of plain hell", but that Helena has made it worse. Helena's response is simply to assert authority over Alison, who now is "numbed and vague" (p. 60), so that when Jimmy asks Alison (with "eyes burning into her") to go with him to the bedside of a dying woman friend, she denies him—moving instead to the sound-cue of church bells (like the servant responding to the speaking-tube on the last page of Strindberg's *Miss Julie*). Jimmy has lost. Throwing his bear downstage—where it rattles and groans in falling—he collapses on his bed in despair.

Scene Two of Act II—the play's slow movement—consists largely of Alison's discussion with her sympathetic father. Both male and born to the life Jimmy is searching for, his reflection that Alison likes "to sit on the fence because it's comfortable and more peaceful" (p. 66) is hard to argue against. Alison calls Jimmy a "spiritual barbarian" who thought he had a "genius for love and friendship" (p. 67), yet she almost breaks down and stays after all—as if she accepted his own assessment after everything that has happened. She does leave the squirrel as a token of self, her resolve to leave being firmed up only by Helena's return (p. 68). Cliff and Alison agree that Alison is being "conventional" in leaving without seeing Jimmy again;

instead, she leaves a note repeating her wish for "peace" (pp. 70, 72). When Jimmy returns, upset over his deathbed vigil, he refuses to be "overcome with awe because that cruel, stupid girl is going to have a baby!" (which Helena has finally told him). The scene ends with Helena—who has telegraphed the action moments before by lying down on the bed while clasping the bear to herself—responding to Jimmy's epithet ("evil-minded little virgin") with a slap, then a passionate, bed-bound kiss. Yet Jimmy feels only "pain" and "despair" (pp. 72-4).

What to make of Jimmy and his women? That his wild energy attracts them is clear enough, but what of his feelings towards them? Even the aforementioned Madeline, Cliff says, was "nearly old enough to be his mother" (p. 71). Does he not need of them, far more than simply sex, an emotional completion that will release him from immaturity, from arrested development?

It would seem so. When Act III opens with a deliberate variation on the play's beginning—this time with Helena in place "months later" as contented mistress of the household—there is a new theme in the newspapers that Jimmy reads. News of fertility rituals in the Midlands, complete with blood sacrifices, leads Jimmy to propose sacrificing Cliff and making "a loving cup from his blood" (pp. 76-7). Jimmy's thoughts on sacrifice are worth quoting in full:

> . . . After all the whole point of a sacrifice is that you give up something you never really wanted in the first place. You know what I mean? People are doing it around you all the time. They give up their careers, say—or their beliefs—or sex. And everyone thinks to themselves: how wonderful to be able to do that. If only I were capable of doing that! But the truth of it is that they've been kidding themselves, and they've been kidding you. It's not awfully difficult—giving up something you were incapable of ever really wanting . . .
>
> (pp. 76-7)

Lest we miss the application, Jimmy begins to ask Helena some questions. Is she "going to Church?" Doesn't she look "satanic"? Does she feel "sinful"? Jimmy's teasing extends to wondering whether he himself needs "some of this spiritual beefcake", and with more references to Eliot, he and Cliff begin another of their music hall routines—this one heavily dependent on sexual content (pp. 78-80). Helena attempts to join in, and also to wash Cliff's dirty shirt; but Cliff, who readily handed Alison his trousers in Act I, now hesitates (p. 83). Something isn't right, and Jimmy is willing to let Cliff leave, much as he loves his friend. Jimmy laments that the big causes are all over with, that there is nothing to bleed for now, nothing to do "but to let yourself be butchered by the women" (pp. 84-5). But where is the battle, now that these former enemies are lovers? And where is life, now that the struggle has disappeared from view?

It is as though John Osborne thinks women necessary, at least dramatically, for the conflict they provide. Jimmy's restless energy, his desire for violent body-contact, has for the last time included Cliff, who feels "wrong" in Helena's company as he never had with Alison. Now he warns Helena, to whom he is physically tender, that "when people put down their weapons, it doesn't mean they've necessarily stopped fighting." Like a "victorious general" sick of the fray, he is at rest in her arms, and even making plans to move, change jobs, etc. Yet he warns her not to "let anything go wrong", because he has put himself into her hands, accepting "peace", which is inimical to him. He is a fighter who needs conflict, and requires a source of strength at home. Instead, uncharacteristic softness and conventional ambitions—respectability—hold sway; he will ride with the system, not threaten it. In his most self-consciously Christlike line, he says to Helena, "Either you're with me or against me" (pp. 86-7). It is indeed a warning: the commitments must be total, or else the war will resume.

While Jimmy plays his trumpet offstage, Alison and Helena begin the final scene. Ironically, the wife feels guilty for intruding upon Jimmy and Helena—not because of "the divine rights of marriage", but rather because of their mutual "consent". Alison's presence underscores the differences between the two women: Helena feels *"ashamed"*, acknowledging Alison's rights and saying she has always known what she did was "wrong", "wrong and evil" (pp. 88-90). But Alison agrees with Helena's assessment of Jimmy as "futile" (a key word here), an anachronism. Helena continues to believe in "good and evil", even thinking that Alison's loss of

120

her baby is "like a judgment on us" (p. 91). Helena speaks conventional morality, while Alison talks of logic—yet Alison knows what an improbable combination of types the right woman for Jimmy would have to be.

That type is not Helena, who now leaves saying that "you can't be happy when what you're doing is wrong, or is hurting someone else"; besides, she doesn't want to "take part—in all this suffering" (p. 93). Like Hedda Gabler, she rejects what is for Jimmy the essence of life—its totality, the sordid and negative included. Says Jimmy, "They all want to escape from the pain of being alive. And, most of all, from love" (p. 93). The church bells start to toll again. Love, he goes on, "takes muscle and guts"; it is a messy operation at best, and if you can't stand it, "you'd better give up the whole idea of life, and become a saint . . . Because you'll never make it as a human being. It's either this world or the next" (pp. 93-4).

This existential focus John Osborne finally brings his play to is the figure of a Christ for the here-and-now, lonely, "like the old bear", and needing someone who knows how to "relax"— because "you've got to be really brawny to have that kind of strength—the strength to relax" (pp. 93-5). And Alison answers Jimmy's speech with her own, matching Jimmy's deed for wish: she doesn't want to be "neutral", or a "saint"; she wants instead to be "a lost cause", "corrupt and futile". Because her loss has finally placed her "in the fire", and in her martyr's burning she found herself finally low, human, and— almost impossibly—just what Jimmy had asked for, she now "relaxes suddenly" (pp. 95-6). It is completed.

If we remember that these loving final speeches are given "with a kind of mocking, tender irony", we will realise that Jimmy and Alison never simply return to the world of squirrels and bears, the world of their earlier immaturity. Their awareness of the "cruel steel traps" awaiting "rather mad, slightly satanic, and very timid little animals" (p. 96) suggests that being "futile" together necessarily involves a plan of action, else why this awareness of threat? If nothing is ventured, whence comes loss? However immature Osborne's sense of religiosity, he dramatizes a nuclear process by which a tremendous energy is seen welling up at his play's conclusion.

The reciprocity in the new alliance of Jimmy Porter and the

altered version of Alison marks a radical change at the ending of *Look Back in Anger*. Though Osborne does not, in any prophetic detail, look forward beyond the limits of the play, nor even hint at change (as Odets might have), neither does the work present any evidence to contradict the view that Jimmy Porter will at last grow up, now that he has what he had always asked for. When all the odds have been changed, we are foolish to bet on stasis. Putting it another way, why should an "angry" play conclude on a note of despair when despair has long since been available, and under less propitious circumstances?

Jimmy Porter, this character who "thinks he's still in the middle of the French Revolution" (p. 90), could make real change in modern English life. In presenting his protagonist, John Osborne uses the model of Christ and "improves" upon it: completes it with the harmonics of a loving (albeit conflict-prone) relationship, gives it a focus in the here-and-now, and makes it morally innovative—not subservient to the prescriptive ethics of institutional churches. Ten years later, John Lennon and Paul McCartney would write "A Day in the Life", and set the themes of Jimmy Porter's newspaper musings to music. Twenty years after, and more, the rhetoric of John Osborne's play—everything below a rant, above a sigh—looks hollow in the hindsight of sold-out revolts and committed churches. Never mind: we will find the play poetic enough when we plumb the depth of our need—and note our vacant cross.

NOTE

A version of this chapter first appeared in the Canadian journal *Ariel*, with whose kind permission it is now reprinted here in revised form.

1   John Osborne, *Look Back in Anger* (London, 1955). All page references appear parenthetically within my text.

9

Williams'
Sweet Singer of Sex:
Orpheus Descending

So permeated are the works of Tennessee Williams with Christ-patternings that we might well take any of his plays as exemplars, though we can hardly omit him from consideration. As obvious as the Christ-imagery of *Orpheus Descending* (1957)[1] is, it is also—thanks to the talents of the playwright—by no means the only pattern of imagery in this much-discussed play. Moreover, though the play is a dubious success, thanks to the dominance of these same systematized patternings, we can at least discuss it as a representative example in the hope of shedding further light on the Christ presence's significance in Williams' work generally. The intermingling of the myths of Orpheus and Eurydice and of Persephone with the narrative of Christ provides the play, with its otherwise slender gifts, with a richness of literary resonance to flesh out its aesthetic substance.

But "slender" "substance" is a description there is no point in retreating from or arguing around: take away the myths from beneath *Orpheus Descending*, and there is precious little left—though the play moves along well enough for the literate and tolerant theatregoer. Perhaps that observable fact is, in a way which is its own excuse for being, an argument for the abiding power of myth on the modern stage—for a novel like *Ulysses*, as Anthony Burgess has recently remarked, could well have succeeded on its own abundant merits without any titular hintings for the academically clever to feast upon. Drama is seldom so luckily indebted to a single overmastering and informing mythical pattern that it can survive on that basis alone, yet it is always the fortunate recipient of drama's inherent gift of nature: the sheer believability of whatever happens on whatever is dubbed a stage by whoever are deputed to be actors; the overwhelming is-ness of what can be plainly *seen* and *heard*.

Hence a powerful cast can rescue *Orpheus* from burdens placed upon them by the play's quick scenes and slightness of characterisation. What do we know about Val, or Lady, or Jabe? Simply that he or she "stands for" some certain figure in a classic myth. Is that all? Well, not exactly, though the additional materials we are furnished with do not amount to much that is worth studying. They are simply local colour, and no whit more demanding than the expository matter customarily delivered to the audience of that expired and once peculiarly American literary sub-genre. We start to speak of *Orpheus Descending* with our work cut out for us: that is, already patterned and needing only the piecing-together and the basting and the final sewing-up.

When the play opens, the "nonrealistic" set shows us a southern store with an inner room, a "confectionery" that is "shadowy and poetic as some inner dimension of the play" (p. 227). It is rainy outside the house of—the name provides emphasis—Torrance; and while rain can be depressing, it also represents a "natural" release of energies, a renewal in the form of a promise, an annual redemption from the desert Waste Land. We must not be surprised to discover that the bedroom of this set is masked by an "Oriental drapery" bearing "the formal design of a gold tree with scarlet fruit and fantastic birds" (p. 227). This is a Garden we can all remember having visited.

But Death is upon the land: Jabe Torrance cannot survive long; indeed, he continues to exist on the sufferance of others (pp. 228-29). Lady had a previous affair with "that Cutrere boy" before being "bought" by old Jabe Torrance. Her father was "a Wop from the old country" with a "mandolin and a monkey that wore a little green velvet suit" (p. 230). When Lady and her lover came together they "made a fire!—yes—fire" (p. 230). And the "Wop's" confectionery had been the lovers' favourite meeting-place in those days, until after the Wop made the mistake of selling "liquor to niggers" there was a sudden and mysterious fire which consumed the premises, the owner being *"burned alive"* (p. 232). Now Lady is married to one of those who murdered her father, though she does not know it yet. She plans to re-open the confectionery "the Saturday before Easter this spring!", in spite of Jabe's illness (pp. 234-35). This is all very ominous matter, the result of Williams' conscious shouldering of the burden of a literary myth. Thus the "Prologue" ends, the audience having been given enough to proceed on—and certainly an inkling of the play's mythic foundation.

Moving from the Prologue into the play's first regular scene, we are immediately introduced to Carol Cutrere—her salient personal characteristics, her headstrong fulfilment of the knowledge that "she's a Cutrere!" (pp. 236-37). She is also possessed of "an odd, fugitive beauty", and the authorial description insures our accepting her as one of Williams' pilgrims of love, yearning exiles from its Garden. There is an element of the "fantastic" about her make-up, underscoring her self-consciously dramatic function within the play and the lives of its characters. Moreover, she is followed on stage by the Conjure Man, whose eerie presence drives the significantly-named Temple sisters away (pp. 239-40).

The Conjure Man, a figure out of voodoo cult-worship, is an example of the sort of literary grotesquery that is possible to the writer from the American South who wishes to utilize the materials of his native region in writing for outlanders; as has been frequently noted with regard to southern fiction-writers, such grotesque creation succeeds because readers are willing to suspend normal criteria of credibility in the belief that no form of behaviour or incident is too bizarre to occur in such a place as the American South. To some extent, of course, this condition is simply a reflection of northern prejudice. This is not to argue against the credibility of the Conjure Man as he appears here, but rather to note the way in which the dramatic representation of mythic patterns is assisted by more than the above-noted "is-ness" of drama. The Conjure Man produces "the breastbone of a bird" as a fetish, but Carol—who is on terms of communication with the Conjure Man—rejects the offering because it is still "tainted with corruption"—one of the play's rallying cries. Though now it is merely a "black charm", when burned and washed clean by sun and rain it will become "a good charm, a white charm". One assumes that Carol is not revealing her own racism here, but rather that Williams is speaking of universal symbols being created. (One thinks, perhaps, of the distribution of Grandier's bones in *The Devils*.) The exchange is completed by Carol's leading the Conjure Man into the barking "Choctaw cry" (p. 240), a significant moment in a play which makes many references to dogs and even has a character called Dog in it (compare *The Wild Duck*); but the moment "works" for us because we do not know enough to take exception to it if we would. This extraordinary and chilling cry, importantly, brings on stage the character of Val.

Perhaps it requires a Choctaw cry to introduce a figure like Val. His Orphic function suggested by a guitar autographed by various folk musicians, he is "a young man, about 30, who has a kind of wild beauty about him that the cry would suggest" (p. 240). In other words, given what we have noted thus far in other plays, Val is a likely candidate for human sacrifice. He also wears a "remarkable garment", "a snakeskin jacket" which is to remain his distinctive badge—of office, as it were. For the snake has long been associated with primitive cult magic of all sorts, including that practised by certain Christian bodies in the more remote regions of the American South. The snake has long been linked with healing and, through its supposed regenerative powers (skin-shedding), with the renewal accomplished within the two or three myths we are discussing in this chapter. The snake is one of the most curious of Christ-symbols, considering the role of the serpent in Eden; yet by a short extension of *felix culpa* thinking, it is possible to envision the snake as a fore-runner of Christ, for the one makes possible the eventual salvation of mankind which the other accomplishes by sacrifice of self. Lastly, the snake is apparently the focal image by which, historically, the worships of Christ and Orpheus have been at least temporarily united.

While we watch this interesting new character, the painter Vee talks about her work—which leaves her feeling "burned out" afterwards, "elevated" (p. 241). Thus while Val is standing there for inspection, the themes he is meant to embody are presented directly to the audience. Moreover, Vee has been working on a painting of "the Holy Ghost ascending"; instead of a head the painting shows a "blaze of light" (p. 242). The Holy Ghost is more usually presented as a bird and associated with sanctification, or regenerative spirituality—which nicely suits the bird/snake/dog image-set of the play, as well as its more abstract representations. Note also the version of the Orpheus legend in which he is finally beheaded. Williams does not seem bothered by an notional clash between Holy Ghost and Christ/Son, for he has emphasised the latter connection by naming Val Xavier, thus "Saviour". But it was an evangelising St. Francis who bore that second name; Val's first, on the other hand, reminds us of St. Valentine, a saint associated with the feast of love (for no apparent reason, except for the British legend that birds chose their mates on what became his feast-day). A Christian saint whose day is a lovers' holiday, nonetheless, is by no great stretching of our imaginations a kind of Christian love-god. The historical Valentine was Italian (like Lady's people), a doctor (a profession with the snake for its symbol), and martyr. And though Val denies it, Carol says that she and he had met before, when he was wearing "a snake ring"—and that their discussion had included her conclusion, an apparent result of his influence at the moment, that "what on earth can you do but catch at whatever comes near you with both your hands until your fingers are broken" (pp. 244-45). And Val is tremendously aware that he is thirty, "not young any more", and apparently obliged to think of a more serious mission in life (p. 246). Having established this complicated and interweaving set of dramatic resonances, Williams is ready to bring on his Eurydice.

A somewhat older woman "who met with emotional disaster in her girlhood", Lady is clearly under considerable strain even now; yet she also shows a capacity for acting and seeming considerably younger. Her "gaunt, wolfish" husband Jabe is along, seeming to stand for Death itself (p. 247); for though he calls out "Jesus" in his exhaustion and reminds us of his presence from time to time by knocking on the floor above, Jabe is already in Death's camp—his situation hopeless, his presence corrupting. Yet it is about Carol that there are whispers that she is "corrupt"; but the townsfolk are mistaken: Carol may be a "benign exhibitionist", but what she flaunts in their faces is her life-commitment, her desperate siding with the forces of Life itself (pp. 250-51). She even visits the cemetery just to hear the dead people tell her their one-word message, "Live . . ." (p. 252). As the strands of the plot are tucked into place and the first scene concludes, the values weighed by the play have all been set forth for our appraisal, each one clearly embodied by an appropriate character.

Act I, Scene Two, therefore, can set these characters into their dance of metaphor together. Val enters the darkened store after his evening with Carol, muttering "Christ" and wiping her lipstick off his face; he moves for his guitar as Lady enters with her ancient dog Bella (p. 256). Needing medicine to help her to sleep, she too is calling on Christ—and the local pharmacist—for assistance (p. 258). Carol has already attempted to make use of Val's services—as "Male at Stud", as he puts it sarcastically (p. 258). Now it is Lady's turn; handling his snakeskin jacket, she remarks upon its unusual warmth, and Val reveals that—"Stud" or not—his temperature, like a dog's, is always at a higher "normal" than other people's are (p. 259). Lady slips his jacket on (compare this with the actions of the village girls in Synge's *Playboy*), and Val talks about himself and his attitudes—he does "electric repairs" for a living—in a passage worth quoting for the way it brings the play's operating themes together:

> VAL: . . . I can do all kinds of odd jobs. Lady, I'm thirty today and I'm through with the life that I've been leading. [*Pause. Dog bays in distance.*] I loved in corruption but I'm not corrupted. Here is why. [*Picks up his guitar.*] My life's companion! It washes me clean like water when anything unclean has touched me . . . [*Plays softly, with a slow smile.*]
>
> (p. 261)

Val has a reputation for being strange, is possessed of extra-ordinary physical self-control, and "can burn down a woman" if he wants to (p. 264). And with an exchange about how some people are bought and sold in this world, he and Lady enter into a phase of deeper conversational complicity. Val speaks of a kind of legless bird that never lands but rather spends its whole life in the air, up in a rarified atmosphere, and does not come down again until it dies. An epitome of freedom, it must be

128

"God's . . . perfect creature", Lady avers; she, like Val, would like to be "one of those birds and never be—corrupted!" (p. 266). And thus Val is hired, leaving his guitar in the store as a sign of trust in Lady, whom he praises—as a dog barks in the distance. If she has any more trouble sleeping, she is to come to him, for he has learned a trick with the "neck and spine" that a lady osteopath once taught him to perform (p. 267). But Val has already begun to do his work: the legless bird is flying; (remember *The Wild Duck* and *The Seagull* and their title-images) and she laughs now "as lightly and gaily as a young girl". When the curtain falls, she is—rather like Helena in Osborne's *Look Back in Anger*—seen running her hands "tenderly over his guitar" (p. 267).

As Act II begins, we see Lady, already jealous, reacting to Val's telling about another woman who had designs on him, and to whom he had to point out that valentines were superfluous, for his "*name* is Valentine" (pp. 268-69). Lady notes that everything Val does is "suggestive", and when he offers to leave, he defines their relationship as being "like a couple of animals sniffin' around each other" (pp. 269-70). Val had once thought that people got to know one another by touching each other, but now he thinks that "we're under a lifelong sentence to solitary confinement inside our own lonely skins for as long as we live on this earth!" (pp. 270-71). If you wait long enough, you get the "make-believe answer": "Love" (pp. 271-72). After Val had followed a naked girl back in the bayou country "like a bird's tail follows a bird", he decided he had been "corrupted"—which was no answer (pp. 272-73).

Carol enters, desperate as "a wild animal at bay", and—left alone with Val—desires to touch him, to hold something with the same "tender protection" he accords his guitar (pp. 277, 280-81). He notes the frailty of her wrist bone, the transparency of her skin; "little bird", he calls her, advising her to "fly away" before something bad happens to her (pp. 281-82). Carol returns the warning, saying that his new captivity (now that his snakeskin jacket is off) is a source of danger to him. With that, her brother David bursts in; he is a man wearing hunter's clothes and having the look of a man whose "power is that of a captive who rules over other captives" (pp. 282-83). When Lady and David are left on stage alone together, she reveals that

129

she had once carried—then aborted—his child, for he preferred a marriage of social convenience; thus both of them had been bought and sold by this transaction, which took place during the summer of the burning of Lady's wine garden (pp. 284-85). Thus Lady entrapped herself, cutting herself off from both father and child; and now she has only the hope of a restored wine garden-confectionery left (pp. 286-87). The scene ends with Lady's stated intention of returning to "life" again.

But the price of such renewal is suggested to be more than mortals can bear—the effect of a blinding, flaming light, such as the one (the setting sun) which has momentarily blinded Vee as Scene Two starts. A discussion of vision leads to Vee showing Val her painting of a "Church of the Resurrection" which has an unnaturalistic red steeple because Vee "just *felt* it that way!" Vee calls herself a visionary: "You've got to have—*vision*—to *see!*" Williams of course intends no mere statement of the self-evident, for this conversation affects Val deeply; the two agree that painting's form of vision has been a way of making sense of existence (pp. 288-90). And both of them have seen "awful things", including the violence inflicted on fugitives—Val noting that there are slower forms of violence too, such as corruption, the rotting of "men's hearts" (p. 291). Then Val, completing a scene of rather greater introspection than we have thought him capable of till now, moves to kiss Vee's fingers—fingers which have made beauty out of "this dark country", as if God had touched them (p. 292). The scene ends with an angry husband's intrusion; Val's instinctive recourse is to play his guitar.

Lady now enters. The impetus of the preceding scene is carried onward by the offstage noise of dogs running down a fugitive, making understandable a certain air of desperation. Thus Lady's next act is to invite Val to stay in the room with the fantastic curtain—which is now illuminated for us from behind (pp. 294, 296). Rather operatic, in the Menotti manner, the brief scene ends with Lady thinking Val a thief, for he has borrowed cash from the cash register and fled into the night. Yet there has also been a moment of mutual "relaxing", as Val again puts into effect his technique for muscular tension—a strange bit of foreshadowing that also recalls Osborne's play (pp. 298-300). Val brings back the cash, and himself, in the next

scene, chiding Lady for her wanting him to "do double duty"—
to work as "a store clerk days and a stud nights" (p. 304). She
denies this violently ("Oh, God no") and then shouts—to stop
him from leaving, "spreading her arms like a crossbar over the
door"—"NO, NO, DON'T GO . . . I NEED YOU!!! . . . TO
LIVE . . . TO GO ON LIVING!!!" Thus the fated assignation
takes place, with Val overcoming what remains of her
resistance by whispering the words of "Lady's Love Song"
while accompanying himself on guitar. The harrowing of
Lady's personal hell is therefore being brought about by an act
of loving deified, as it were, by allusions to not only the Orphic
myth but also the Christian. It is as if the Garden might be
restored by the snake's curative powers (p. 305). As in Albee's
dramaturgy, love's demands sometimes require to be
shouted—failing which, as many playwrights have noted, it
takes a sacrificial death to bring about love's redemption,
spring's renewal.

Act III, therefore, is specifically set on the "Saturday before
Easter" (p. 306), when ironically Christ himself is in the tomb,
as yet unresurrected. Should the stressing of these Christ-
references seem excessive, and their implications unduly moral,
we might remember that the original version of this play was
called *Battle of Angels*, a title implying moral struggle on a
cosmic scale; there, Val Xavier was pitted against a Jabe
presented as Satanic, not merely as Death. Lady's name in the
original was Myra; the elevation of the name for *Orpheus
Descending* disguises the interesting Freudianism of the fact that
Myra is an anagram for Mary. We may also recall the theme of
the child's rhyme about the "Ladybug"—or "-bird"—who is
sent home because her house is on fire, her children in danger of
burning; it is only a short while since Val urged Carol, as "little
bird", to "fly away" before it was too late (pp. 281-82).

The sacrificial event is threatened by Jabe's attempt to come
downstairs, causing Lady to urge Val, "Jesus, will you get up
and put some clothes on?" (p. 306). To further the dramatic
irony of the situation, Jabe appears in his black suit, "bizarre
and awful" as a "brilliant shaft of light" from the sun falls on his
person (p. 307). This "miracle" of his descent is undercut by his
appearance, for he sits staring into the light "like a fierce dying
old beast" (pp. 307-8). With Lady calling on God and

131

comparing the day to the day before Christmas, Val notes that Jabe "looks like death", while the latter finds the newly-decorated confectionery "artistic as hell" (pp. 309-11). Lady chortles that she hired the calliope playing outside "for a song" to advertise the event, but Jabe is shrewd enough to inquire, "How much of a song did you hire it for?" (p. 312). Jabe may only suspect what sort of music was played behind the Garden-curtain, but he does use the moment to reveal—finally, maliciously, and callously—that he had participated in the killing of Lady's father (pp. 312-13). His statement helps to foreshadow Val's end, of course—for Val is, along with blacks, foreigners, artists and all lovers and visionaries, a part of the "fugitive kind" who are enemies to the likes of Jabe.

Scene Two continues to enforce this theme. Val is seen waiting apprehensively "in the tense, frozen attitude of a wild animal listening to something that warns it of danger"; and Vee enters "*struck blind!*" by a road-to-Damascus vision of the Risen Christ she has just had (pp. 314-16). "TWO HUGE BLAZING EYES OF JESUS CHRIST RISEN" have burned themselves into her consciousness, and she has had the sensation of having been touched on her "great heaving bosom" by the hand of the Christ; as she tells Val of the event, she presses his hand to that selfsame bosom—just in time for her husband to witness and misinterpret the deed (p. 316). Vee collapses against Val, seeing still in her mystic's vision the eyes of Christ; and both literal and symbolic levels of the play begin their rush to fulfilment. The men threaten Val, and handle his guitar (p. 319); his response is a catlike leap towards freedom (compare *Playboy*). Warned to be out of the county by Easter morning, Val ends the scene by playing the "Dog Howl Blues" in the sunset's "fiery afterglow" as dogs howl in the background. Tensions are resolved by Val's "slight, abrupt nod of his head" (p. 321)—an obvious touch of Christlike resignation.

Scene Three begins even more unrealistically than previous parts of the play, with odd lighting, dogs occasionally howling, and each passer-by moving "like a shade in the under kingdom" (p. 322). Lady appears, dressed to celebrate the opening of the confectionery, the recreation in sweets of the vanished wine garden, and tells the Temple sisters about her father's dancing monkey (pp. 324-25). Carol's entrance is followed by that of the Conjure Man, whom she pays to hear his Choctaw cry; its barking sound has the usual effect, and Val enters on this melodramatic cue (pp. 326-27). "Something is still wild in the country!" Carol exults (p. 327); apparently there is still hope for a southern, or American, land so often bought and sold. Lady asks God's blessing on Val for helping her to stave off defeat by the man upstairs who has already cost her three lives (p. 329). When Val, snakeskin uniform on, prepares to leave, Lady makes him confess her love for her, and demands that he stay. Crazed by the energies released by her liberation, she reveals the truth about herself in a remarkable confession to Val that effectively counters his melodramatic entrance:

> LADY: I know! Death's knocking for me! Don't you think I hear him, knock, knock, knock? It sounds like what it is! Bones knocking bones . . . Ask me how it felt to be coupled with death up there, and I can tell you. My skin crawled when he touched me. But I endured it. I guess my heart knew that somebody must be coming to take me out of this hell! You did. You came. Now look at me! I'm alive once more! [*Convulsive sobbing controlled: continues more calmly and harshly:*]—*I won't wither in dark!* Got that through your skull? . . .
>
> (p. 333)

Death, she has decided, must die.

After some by-play with the Nurse on the subject of mercy-killing (the Nurse arguing that people are not animals), the Nurse discovers a fire in the alcove. Lady's interruptions produce the Nurse's angry accusations as to Lady's infidelity and pregnancy, and for the moment the fire is forgotten (pp. 334-36), as Lady states that her pregnancy has given her "*great—joy!*" What is in effect Lady's Magnificat, then, is ritually blessed by Val's kissing of her fingers as she confesses that "this dead tree, my body, has burst in flower! You've given me life, you can't go!" (p. 337). The significance of such gestures as Val's breathing on Lady's hands is emphasized by Lady's telling a long story about a barren fig tree (an obvious Christian reference) that suddenly bore fruit, whereupon she decorated it as though it were a Christmas tree (pp. 337-38).

133

Christmas and Easter: Lady rushes upstairs to announce her victory, only to recoil as if blinded from the revisitation of Jabe—"Death's self", in a "stained purple robe", who has returned to claim his own (p. 338).

Calling "Buzzards! Buzzards!" as if he were summoning his minions, Jabe fires his revolver into the store; Lady is mortally stricken protecting Val, the breath knocked out of her with a great "*Hah!*" (Much is made, in this play, of the function of breath as a life-principle.) Lady rises for a last look at her confectionery ("The show is over. The monkey is dead . . . ," she utters in another operatic moment), while Val is hauled off by the men (to oaths of "Christ") to a fiery death (pp. 338-41). In the offstage glare of the blue flame of Val's death, Carol purchases Val's snakeskin jacket from the Conjure Man and speaks the play's moral—just before exiting, in contempt of the power of the sheriff to detain her; and as the Conjure Man smiles the "secret smile" of the fugitive kind:

> CAROL: . . . —Wild things leave skins behind them, they leave clean skins and teeth and white bones behind them, and these are tokens passed from one to another, so that the fugitive kind can always follow their own kind . . .
>
> (p.341)

With that—and Val's dying cry—the play comes to a close.

In *Orpheus Descending,* the Christ-figure Val is scarcely fleshed out in the normal sense of characterisation, and yet he intrigues any audience he appears before. The myths through which he operates are so many and so rich that he can hardly fail to do so. Lord of music, of animal spirits, of all that is "fugitive" and exiled, Val is the redeemer of sexuality, the sweet singer terribly aware of the precious gift he possesses, and gifted with sufficient integrity to accept his own, rather than another's, martyrdom. For though Lady dies, it is in spite of, not because of, Val's saving grace: he is a tourist of healthy sexuality, an American— and thus, a vagrant—version of the ministers of the Life Force who so obsessed the dramatists of northern Europe some decades previously. His presence causes others to speak loudly of their visions, his shed skin all the while working its wonders. Val Xavier is, finally, a messenger from another order of creation; as such, he must be put to death, as all such messengers ultimately are. For they rouse us to ourselves.

NOTE

1   Tennessee Williams, *Orpheus Descending*, in *The Theatre of Tennessee Williams*, 3 (New York, 1971). All page references appear parenthetically within my text.

10

Pinter's Christ of Complicity: *The Birthday Party*

In his early play *The Birthday Party* (1958),[1] Harold Pinter presents his audience with the figure of a type of Christ, Stanley, who is in no sense a redeemer yet resembles, in his suffering at the hands of merciless tormentors, the Jesus of the early stages of the Passion narrative. It is interesting that Stanley, in his relative silence and helplessness, thus partakes of the pathos accorded the Christ of the Bible narrative, especially in the scenes in which he is scourged and mocked by the Roman soldiers and his other enemies—all of them representatives of a ponderous power structure that has decided he must be eliminated for the smoother functioning of the system. Yet Stanley, for all the sadness of the spectacle he creates, is clearly far from guiltless of the causes of his own persecution; moreover, he accepts his disciplining with the loss of will to resist or flee that is characteristic of Kafka's K. In other words, by occupying the no man's land between the poles of guilt and paranoia, Stanley can be said to represent a Christ of complicity in his own eventual dismemberment: an almost-willing drainer of his over-flowing cup.

Pinter's plays are often cited for the brilliant exposition of the theme of "menace" they present, and for their knack of realizing stage likeness of all the nameless "theys" whom individuals in modern society choose to make respositories of their corporate and individual fears. Less noticed is the degree of culpability evinced by these same individuals—the ways their conduct in the past is shown as catching up to their present selves. Thus

Pinter's "they" could well be projections of an inner sense of guilt, their menace a mirror-image of other individuals' bad faiths. Thus Stanley, in this light, ought not be seen as suffering the pains afforded those who dare be free, or individual; for if the sins he is to suffer for be Everyman's they are also likely to be his. A reading of this play, which is rather more patently "structured" than Pinter's later drama—but which holds up as a landmark of contemporary theatre nevertheless—provides support for the notion of Stanley as a Christ of complicity.

In certain of its elements, *The Birthday Party* is obviously the development of both *The Room* and *The Dumb Waiter*, early plays with much the same concerns. The small talk between Meg and Petey (pp. 19-22) that opens the play, for instance, can be seen by *Room* light as talking against the void: speech to wish away the real Absence, or the absent Real. Stanley is offstage (p. 20), asleep; yet the presence of two strangers is announced (p. 22) as though it might, from the audience's point of view, mean danger to a character we have not yet even seen. It is the deliberate banality of the opening conversation, of course, that renders "the arrival of the stranger(s)" awful; in a conventional play, the busy chatter of butler and maid would likely have made such entrances manageable parts of this, the fabric of the morning. But this is a "straight show", the term Petey uses to describe the "new show coming to the Palace"; there is to be "no singing or dancing", presumably Stanley's forte. This speech-drama will give us pause; its dialogue certainly does (p. 22). Our Stanley plays piano, but he does not sing—"of course" (p. 22). A certain amount of failure to communicate, to fully participate, is taken for granted with Stanley.

The love play offstage between Stanley and Meg, who goes upstairs to rouse him, is part of the reality Petey chooses to ignore, at least at this point—if it can be argued that he notices it at all. But it is also an ostensible part of the initial situation of Stanley's guilt (pp. 23-4). Certainly Stanley is, at this point, rather an assertive presence in his host's household; he has the confidence of the self-satisfied lover (pp. 24-5), complaining about the food and generally expecting favoured treatment. When Petey pushes off to work, it is to leave Meg victim to Stanley's taunts about her house's popularity—though she reminds him that the house is "on the list" in a way that manages to sound ominous—and to sexual by-play over the word "succulent" (pp. 26-7). There is some doubt over whether or not Stanley managed to sleep the night before—the question of prior guilt thus being tossed into the air and suspended there—and the reference by Meg to the "lovely afternoons" she has spent in Stanley's room, with Meg "sensual" and Stanley self-confident (pp. 28-9), creates a moment of initial dramatic exposition that is not to be repeated.

This moment is immediately shattered with Meg's disclosure that "two gentlemen" have arrived and wish to stay there; an immediately apprehensive Stanley reacts with a nervous questioning, and also with a change of heart about the quality of Meg's tea (pp. 30-1). He calls Meg to him, and asks her if she knows who he is (clear, but concededly minor, echoes of the Christ-narrative). His uncertainty leads directly into reminiscence of an ambiguous sort about his career as a pianist (pp. 31-3); there are references to his vaguely defined relationship with his father, as well as to a concert for which the hall was found to be "shuttered up" when Stanley arrived. These memories cause Stanley to take his glasses off and clean them while he "bitterly" describes his refusal to "crawl" (p. 33). (Refusal to see, even in an act so literal as this gesture of Stanley's, is of course a running theme in Pinter's plays.) But when Meg wonders whether Stanley's problem is one of simple constipation, he turns on her, threatening her in terms obviously foreshadowing Albee's use of the same device (in *The American Dream* [1961]) with the arrival of a "van" that contains a wheelbarrow—surely a means of having her somehow taken away. This attempt, which predictably fails, also marks Stanley's last full assertion of his former untroubled state.

The entrance of Lulu confirms Stanley's loss of grace. She complains of the stuffiness, of Stanley's needing of a shave, and of his general lethargy (p. 35). He can only make suspicious claims to having had a morning swim, and then resist Lulu's proposals that they go for a walk together:

> LULU: So you're not coming out for a walk?
> STANLEY: I can't at the moment.
> LULU: You're a bit of a washout, aren't you?

(p. 36)

Stanley is left feeling unmanned, and in need of a face-wash.

Except in a dramatic sense, Stanley is now totally unprepared for the arrival of his tormentors, Goldberg and McCann—the former of whom is clearly in charge. Indeed, so diffident and unsure of himself has he become that he slips out of the back door at the very sight of their backs (p. 37). Though Goldberg is running things, it is McCann who inspires the greater audience fear, thanks to Pinter's management of stage business. At this early point, Goldberg impresses us chiefly with his constant reminiscing about his family's past—a trait by which he also parodies Stanley. McCann, on the other hand, is caught up in his own mysterious agonies—again resembling Stanley. "Everywhere you go these days it's like a funeral", says Goldberg to McCann, and the latter agrees—leaving the audience wondering how many meanings to ascribe to the statement (p. 38). "You've always been a true Christian", observes McCann to Goldberg (p. 39), and Goldberg agrees: "In a way." Again, the remark underscores the disconcerting irony of the scene's dialogue. When Meg returns, we find that Stanley is the focus of their questioning of her (p. 41). Together the two men do seem to constitute a Judeo-Christian conspiracy against Stanley. The self-conscious Hebraisms of Goldberg—his consistent awareness of himself *as* Jew, his familial obsessions, his racial preoccupations—make him a deliberately stereotyped figure, as do McCann's religio-political Hibernianisms. To go further: the two men, apparently borrowed from O'Neill's *The Iceman Cometh*, are surely meant to suggest twin paths of religious (that is, spiritual) oppression—the Old and New Testaments personified.

To put things another way: the visit of Goldberg and McCann seems to be, in its parody of establishment Judeo-Christianity, an apt, if sardonic, reminder of the values Stanley is being held accountable to, and which he presumably has transgressed. Both Goldberg and McCann possess the most negative of features of what are almost vaudeville stereotypes of the Jew and the Irishman, with little genuine redeeming charm. Goldberg is in charge because he is a parody-patriarch, ready to correct a wayward and naughty child. McCann is there to assist him by holding forth a hand empty of conventional Christian

139

mercy; rather, he proffers narrow sectarian concerns with a fatal commitment to a cause. In some way not defined but taken for granted, Stanley has transgressed the Code these gentlemen enforce; with them on the scene, attempts at conventional exposition are bound to be helpless. Stanley now finds himself part of the bitter joke about the Jew, the Irishman, and the piano player.

The combining of Christmas and Easter found in Arden's *Serjeant Musgrave's Dance* and in Williams' *Orpheus Descending* can be said to exist here as well: that the day of Stanley's perverse resurrection from (or to) the dead is also the day of his Nativity—his birthday—is disclosed by Meg, though news to Stanley (p. 42). What luck, though; now Goldberg and McCann can join in the festivities. The latter is described by the former as "the life and soul of any party", to which McCann responds with a startled "What?" (p. 43). But if it is hard enough to think of McCann as any party's "soul", the very name of Goldberg is enough to make Stanley slump into his chair (p. 45). The savage parody, the cruel mockery, of what is appropriate or desirable is continued when Meg—out of consideration for a musician who lacks a piano—gives him a toy drum instead. The piano, we have been led to believe, somehow figures in the story of Stanley's past, and is presumably involved in the narrative of his unspecified guilt; and so the drum, which Stanley hangs around his neck at once, albatross-like, becomes the perverse medium of his guilt's expression, the aural witness of his sense of oncoming disaster, of retribution looming just ahead. Act I now ends with Stanley playing the drum— regularly at first, then eccentrically, and finally frenziedly (p. 46). At the end of his tether, Stanley does not really try to flee; is it because his time is simply up? Because his father's business now must be achieved?

One thinks, perhaps, of all those Biblical parables which centre around great feasts given by kings and heads of households, and especially of the one given for the erring and repentant youth now gathered back into the fold. One thinks as well, perhaps, of sacrifice's central place in stories told of feasts of just this sort. Due ceremony is called for, even if its nature is mysterious and threatening: the very sight of McCann tearing newspapers into strips of carefully-measured size is enough to

make Stanley head for the nearest exit (p. 47). But McCann
stops him, and begins to impress upon Stanley the need for due
respect for his own birthday's importance (pp. 47-9). "It's all
laid on", McCann promises, or threatens; in this feast in which
the fatted animal and the returning prodigal are one and the
same, we might consider how savagely Pinter resolves the
duality of Christ's roles as good shepherd and sacrificial lamb.
Stanley attempts another escape (p. 49), and his gambit of
suggesting that he has McCann's number—that he knows him
from somewhere, sometime, before—fails utterly. Thus Stanley
is forced to try a strategic withdrawal: he speaks of his intention
of returning home, where he would be free of the call of the
"little private business" that has brought him to Meg and
Petey's (p. 50). He denies being the sort to cause any "trouble",
but admits to having been drinking (p. 50); but McCann denies
him any understanding, warning him a second time about
touching his torn newspapers. Stanley tries to portray Meg as
mad for having mistaken the date of his birthday, then becomes
himself nearly hysterical in trying to persuade McCann that he
is innocent. He even resorts to absurd blanket praise of Ireland
and things Irish, including the policeman, the sunsets, and the
draft Guinness (p. 52). But nothing works; McCann is
merciless.

Then Goldberg enters, talking to Petey. Goldberg's dialogue
throughout the play is a wonderfully effusive mixture of family
trivia and *schmaltz*; initially, he is discussing his mother, but
slips immediately into a reverie about the Sunday school
teacher he used to date. He rejects McCann's implied
brotherhood—when the latter suggests that the sun going down
behind Goldberg's dog stadium was like a similar scene in
Carrikmacross (p. 53)—but he immediately introduces another
memory of his mother (to which we shall return). This reference
is part of a pattern in Goldberg's speech—one running on for
several pages consists largely of contrasts between the beauty of
new beginnings and of childhood as against the disgusting
features of a more advanced age (pp. 53-5). During this
onslaught, Stanley tries desperately to maintain an exterior
firmness, but in the end he finally gives in to the threatening
presences of Goldberg and McCann (pp. 56-7).

As the name "Goldberg" contains the sound-suggestion of

"God", McCann, that parody of Christian values, hails from Carrikmacross—a real place, but one which Pinter may have chosen for its aural suggestiveness: "Carry-my-cross." Given McCann's local, especially Catholic, habits of reference, and the disclosure that he is an unfrocked priest with a penchant for confessions, one can readily understand the possibility that Pinter uses their mock-religious associative institutionalism to strengthen their attack upon Stanley. Even as father-and-son in crime, they remind us of the relationship at which Stanley seems to have somehow failed.

At any rate, the interrogation scene which ensues involves the snatching-away of Stanley's glasses (p. 59), an allusion to what has already been noted as a favourite Pinter metaphor. The scene ends:

> GOLDBERG. Your bite is dead. Only your pong is left.
> McCANN. You betrayed our land.
> GOLDBERG. You betray our breed.
> McCANN. Who are you, Webber?
> GOLDBERG. What makes you think you exist?
> McCANN. You're dead.
> GOLDBERG. You're dead. You can't live, you can't think, you can't love. You're dead. You're a plague gone bad. There's no juice in you. You're nothing but an odour!
>
> (p. 62)

It is surely significant that the attack upon Stanley is at last expressed in terms familiar from other plays studied in this volume: his state of death-in-life; his failure to make more than an indifferent job of the mission of being alive.

And in these remarks and in Stanley's last lunge towards retaliatory action—followed by McCann's calling Stanley "Judas" and drawing attention to his "sweating", "bastard sweatpig" that he is—we have an emphasis on Stanley's supposed physical decline as evidenced by his strong smell and his relative lifelessness (pp. 62-3). And though it is unusual to find two professional hit men criticizing their victim as being unable to love, we must remember that we are not in a real world here, but in the quasi-naturalistic ambience of a Pinter play. The capacity for violence represented by Goldberg and McCann, moreover, stands in the same relationship with

Stanley's deadened state as other, like proportionalities we may observe in other plays considered in this volume. Stanley is a mock-Christ, having grown away from childhood innocence into a world where his pretensions to art or independent action ("business") have corrupted him. The evidence is of a literal sort: his odour is spiritual as well as physical. Whether or not Stanley has actually erred severely, and whether or not Goldberg and McCann are being at all unequivocal in their assessment of him, the dramatic metaphor for his state seems apt enough: it sticks, and his actions are coloured thereby.

But now Meg returns, playing the drum. Worse business is afoot. Meg has transferred her flirtatious behaviour from Stanley to Goldberg, and thus Stanley's betrayal of motherhood, wifehood, is replaced by a *heimische* sort of sexual by-play. Goldberg, after all, has never been able to separate mothers and mistresses. Just as confused is Meg's birthday toast (in which her actual relationship to Stanley is obscured) as is the fact of whether Stanley has actually been "bad" or "good" (pp. 64-5). All this while, a flashlight, or torch, has been held on the face of the "birthday boy" by McCann. Thus a ludicrous sort of halo is apparent around the visage of a most unholy and ghastly Stanley. Stanley is silent, but Lulu nakedly admiring, when Goldberg launches into one of his testimonial speeches—full of slang, local references, pious utterances, and gruff cordiality. The halo returns (pp. 66-7), and Stanley is alone.

His aloneness results from Goldberg's crude approaches to Lulu while McCann carries on with Meg (pp. 68-70). It is a parody of tragic isolation, a parody-Christness, that we see. Goldberg makes a reference to his loving wife that is clearly parallel with, if not identical to, an earlier reference to his mother (pp. 53, 69); both involve ambiguous assertions as to his name—is it "Nat" or "Simey"? As Stanley suffers in silence, the foursome regresses to childhood, to assertedly happier times (pp. 69-71). And in response to a plea for a "love song", McCann sings a song about a contemporary Garden of Eden— one sung, his recitation has it, the night before Paddy Reilly was "stretched" (p. 71). Tree of Eden and gallows-tree are thus merged and confused, as are truth and falsity in the narratives of the past that each character has been relieving him/herself of.

Then who is wife, and who is mother? Who mother, and who the friend? It is time for lights-out, and the return to official blindness: Blind Man's Buff is to be played, as in Ibsen (pp. 71-3). The glasses are broken, and Stanley walks into the drum. He makes assaults on both Meg (p. 74) and, in the dark, Lulu (p. 75). Clearly, Stanley has lost track of both time and reality; his discrimination of past and present guilts has ceased. The drum is heard as his enemies move against him (pp. 75-6), a clever parody of a Shakespearean history play. Act II has ended with the celebration of a ritual re-enactment of Stanley's naughtiness; he has, by means of a mousetrap play, been caught out in his own nasty guilt, and now he shall be taken away and punished.

Act III is a comparatively brief tapering-off of the tension of the preceding Act. It becomes clear that Stanley has been interrogated throughout the night (pp. 77-9), yet Meg is almost exclusively concerned with whether or not there is a wheel-barrow in the car waiting outside (p. 79). If Stanley is some sort of Christ, in other words, we must be approaching his general denial. This denial takes the form of going about one's business—as Meg does when she goes out to do the morning's shopping, asking that Stanley be assured that she "won't be long" (p. 81). Sipping his tea, Goldberg calls her "a good woman. A charming woman. My mother was the same. My wife was identical" (p. 81). The suggestion is clearly that good, ordinary people play a stereotyped role in the casual crucifixions of this world—such as Stanley's, which is to come. It is also to slip into a form of sexual metaphor which Ibsen and Shaw had both found useful. But now McCann comes downstairs, having had enough of the night with Stanley (p. 83), who has been given back his broken glasses, but cannot quite recall how to use them. He will have to be taken to someone for treatment, perhaps a doctor, perhaps "Monty" (pp. 83-4).

Here Goldberg seizes McCann by the throat for taking advantage of the Nat/Simey confusion about his name, and McCann has to beg off with a plea of "Honest to God" (p. 86). After this, a cleavage opens up between the two: as in *The Dumb Waiter*, there is a compliant company-man, ready to do the institution's bidding (Goldberg), and another, less comfortable in his assigned role, who just wants to get things over with. This is the extent of McCann's Christianity, then. Moreover, Goldberg, lost for the moment in a mindstream of credos and begats, can only fall back on a Biblical assertiveness of purpose, and a Biblical ritual of power: he asks McCann for a "a breath of life", after which the play can again proceed (pp. 87-9). Throughout all this, there is Goldberg's consistent emphasis upon family, the performance of assigned services to and for others, and the awareness of one's genealogical roots. But the recital has a futile ring, as though one were reading a similar recitation in a Beckett novel.

Yet the play is able to move forward again. Lulu enters to accuse Goldberg of taking all sorts of advantage of her, further evidence of Goldberg's confusion of feminine roles (pp. 89-90). McCann accuses Lulu of unspecified evils and strongly suggesting that she confess (pp. 90-1); it is here, too, that the revelation that McCann has only been defrocked six months is made. Stanley re-enters, a "new man" according to McCann's description (p. 91). Both Goldberg and McCann now begin to "woo" Stanley—that is, they turn into soothing reassurances all the implied threats of the previous interrogation scene. This process (pp. 92-4) is in the interests, it is said, of trying to "save" Stanley; and promises are made, culminating in a possibly absurd mutual commitment that Stanley will henceforth be able to own "animals" (p. 94). Stanley, of course, is far past such recognitions, and cannot make answer to these generous offers, and Petey's try at intervening is met with a stern invitation to come along and see "Monty" (pp. 95-6). But Petey desists, Stanley is taken away, and the play ends with Petey assuring Meg that Stanley is still "asleep"—at which Meg begins to reminisce, in the manner of *The Room*, about how she had once been the "belle of the ball" (pp. 96-7). And thus Stanley disappears from view.

Stanley has been shattered upon the rock of his own unspecified guilts. They have come for him, Goldberg and McCann, to bring him back to *their* senses: that is, to restore him to righteousness. Whether or not he survives as a sentient animal, much less a thinking person, Stanley will have been brought face to face with his own shortcomings and bad conscience. Failure to observe the rules set forth by the Father, failure to love as defined by the Son: these have been his omissions. But then, he has posed for photographs on the way to Calvary. On the counts of both Old and New observances, dispensations, Stanley seems to deserve his punishment; but on such charges, which of us deserves to escape his whipping; which to evade his taking-away? Who, one might add, does not sometimes play the Hound of Heaven to himself?

NOTE

1 Harold Pinter, *The Birthday Party*, in *Plays: One* (London, 1976). All page references appear parenthetically within my text.

11

Albee's Parabolic Christ: *The Zoo Story*

So obvious is the presence of the Christ-myth in Edward Albee's *The Zoo Story* (1958)[1] that little attempt has been made to carry critical attention past the surface of things. Not only does the play's protagonist's name begin with the initial "J" but he is given a "disciple" named Peter; and references to Jesus and especially to God abound, particularly towards the play's violent conclusion—the act of self-sacrifice in love's name by which Jerry intends to impress his "gospel" upon Peter. So much is patent enough. But *The Zoo Story* rests upon a foundation of Christ-references, and indeed derives its peculiar structure from Jesus's favourite teaching device, the parable. Albee has thus constructed a play as ostensibly didactic as a Brechtian "parable"; he has sacrificed little in the way of dramatic impact in the process.

The structure of *The Zoo Story* is unusual enough, and hardly satisfies academic standards of theatrical technique. Though there are similar events in other plays, particularly of the period (one thinks of Albee's own *The American Dream* or of Arthur Kopit's *Oh Dad, Poor Dad, Mamma's Hung You in the Closet and I'm Feelin' So Sad*), there is hardly a competing example of a play of full one-act length that comes to something like a full dramatic stop for nearly the whole of its middle third, as a single character recites a story with a moral while a second character simply sits and listens. One is tempted to call the play broken-backed; and surely there is something provocative about a work in which two strangers meet, converse for a time, then cease all

147

conversation and even apparent interaction during the one's recital of his "story" about himself and a dog. During this lengthy period, moreover, Jerry is probably lighted by the only light on stage (dropping the other stage lights and placing Jerry under a pin spot is common stage practice in the performing of this play), for what is Peter to do meanwhile, his repertory of dramatic "takes" eventually exhausted, but sit in metaphorical darkness anyway? Finally, it should be noted that only the completion of Jerry's story enables the play to resume its course towards a bloody crisis and operatic denouement.

"Operatic" is, in fact, a suitable term to choose to describe Jerry's lengthy and articulate dying (Albee repeats the device in *Tiny Alice*); and the usage complements one's notions that the play is also, structurally, quite "musical", and can be therefore justified in some degree by means of musical analogy. What have we here but a traditional sonata structure, A-B-A, in which a first theme (or, in this case, variety of action) with its appropriate tempo is stated or introduced, followed by the statement of a contrasting theme (or sort of activity), and then the recapitulation of the introductory motif—but with a difference: the change in our perceptions of A resulting from our interim experience of B? And one remembers, therefore, the history of Albee's evident interest in music and musicians: that *The Death of Bessie Smith*, a melodramatic account of a singer's dying, is dedicated to composer Ned Rorem; that *The American Dream* is dedicated to composer David Diamond; and that in fact *The Zoo Story* is similarly dedicated, this time to composer William Flanagan (1923-1969), a friend who wrote the music for Albee's *The Sandbox*, *The Ballad of the Sad Cafe* (adapted from Carson McCullers' *novella*) and *Malcolm* (adapted from James Purdy's novel), and also once set an early Albee poem, "The Lady of Tearful Regret", to a score for soloists and orchestra. Musicality in the handling of themes, verbal "notes", and general structure can be expected in Albee's plays.

We thus expect *The Zoo Story* to be more than a mere collection of words: an orchestration of sounds; and we are not disappointed. The screams of the final moments of the play refer back, we may say, to the jungle roars of the offstage zoo of the title, as well as to the fierce growls of the dog in Jerry's parable. These sounds are a necessary part of the play; their difference from human speech is Albee's way of emphasizing the play's "message" about love. Note Albee's technique of using an illustrative animal fable—or, more accurately, parable—as a means of reaching an adult consciousness deadened by "real" experience to the child's sense of fantasy, of "play". Thus the play within a play is Albee's—and Jerry's—method of recreating Peter in his Master's image, and is arguably to be counted as a Christian parable. As Jerry says of pornographic playing cards shortly before beginning his story of himself and the dog,

> ... It's that when you're a kid you use the cards as a substitute for real experience, and when you're older you use real experience as a substitute for the fantasy. . .
>
> (p. 32)

And such fantasy, possibility, is the forerunner of love.

The opening stage directions establish Peter's middle-of-the-road conservatism, as well as Jerry's "great weariness" (p. 11); though the two men are almost of an age, there is great contrast between them in terms of their respective adjustments to and gleanings from life. Two facts receive initial emphasis: Jerry's having been to the zoo (which he repeats and then even shouts to Peter), and the fact of Jerry's having thus walked north to his meeting with Peter (pp. 12-13). Both facts work together: the "zoo story" is not what Peter thinks it may be, but instead involves the sermon on animal contact that Jerry intends to deliver, and its pathetic results when Peter fails to understand. The play's harping on geography will reinforce its notion that you must at times go a long way to travel a short distance (indeed, in starting from Greenwich Village to reach a point midway between West Side and East, Jerry arguably traces a cross upon the map of Manhattan [pp. 12-13, 15-16]). Animalistic behaviour is linked, by this foreshadowing, with the idea of strenuous and extreme effort to effect a noble aim, and the play is launched on its course—with or without full audience comprehension.

Animal imagery to express love? The mind expects one or both of two alternative images, abusive violence and/or wild sexuality. If Albee means the latter, he hedges his statement by confining his references largely to the former. Thus while Jerry is allowed to mock Peter's statistically average sex-life (pp. 16-18), what we learn of Jerry's is confined to his sneering at the necessity of marriage (p. 17), telling of his verbally repulsing an overt sexual advance by another male (rather abstractedly, however [p. 19]), and, while an orphan since childhood (p. 28), his now being something of a reformed homosexual:

> ... for a week and a half, when I was fifteen ... and I hang my head in shame that puberty was late ... I was a h-o-m-o-s-e-x-u-a-l. I mean, I was queer ... *(Very fast)* ... queer, queer, queer ... with bells ringing, banners snapping in the wind. And for those eleven days, I met at least twice a day with the park superintendent's son ... a Greek boy ...
>
> (p. 30)

But now, says Jerry, he does "love the little ladies; really, I love them. For about an hour" (p. 30). Jerry's sex-life now apparently consists of encounters with street-walkers, his form of Peter's concession to society's expectations of normality in sexual matters, perhaps. The possible "gayness" of Jerry is introduced into the play for those interested—only to be discarded; readers may see the final tableau and its unwilling penetration of one man's body by another, or interpret a weapon being held by another, as a savage parody of a homosexual encounter—but should not turn the play's values entirely in that direction. For Edward Albee in 1958, *The Zoo Story* would be about a Christ as savage as Synge's *Playboy*'s, but it could not yet be—with other and more general matters to take care of first—ostensibly about a "gay" one.

Just what end Albee has in mind is suggested only by Jerry's beginning to pace about, his personal tensions building up towards the release provided by the telling of the story about himself and the dog (this by explicit authorial design), followed immediately by Jerry's saying that he came to the zoo up Fifth Avenue from Washington Square because "sometimes a person has to go a very long distance out of his way to come back a short way correctly" (pp. 24-5). Jerry thus makes literal the disparity between his world and Peter's, between "West Side" and "East Side"—which at least to the eye of the map-reader are Manhattan's nearest extremes. Arguably, this statement of Jerry's is also a structural apologia for the play. But when Peter and Jerry meet in Central Park, the centrality of which is both literal and ironic (in terms of the worlds to be bridged there), and which is idyllically beautiful in spots and then without as much of a reputation for violence as it now possesses, they meet on neutral ground ("turf" in the parlance of *West Side Story*, a not totally dissimilar exercise) between the territories appropriate to two contrasting lifestyles.

Such neutral ground is required for the meeting of what have almost become two separate species, as it were; Peter's tame existence contrasts vividly with the rooming-house world in which Jerry lives, its inhabitants constituting the cosmos of his imagination: the coloured queen, the Puerto Rican family, the lady who cries all the time (pp. 26, 32-3). Those landmark volumes of Fifties sociology, *The Lonely Crowd* and *The Organization Man,* are quite clearly behind this radical dichotomy of Albee's. And even the defects of his personal possessions may indicate Jerry's own failure to respond to the demands these people place upon him (his empty picture frames, his collection of rocks, his "please letters" [p. 27])— even, perhaps, including the demands of his own seemingly repressed homosexuality, if it is that sort of failure he is referring to. Whatever the full extent of Jerry's guilts, the confessions inherent in his partial revelations, it is certain that his is a nature that feels the burden of being human all around him, however poorly he may have responded thus far, whereas Peter is a character untouched by the claims of others upon his emotions, and may be the sort of indifferent soul to whom—as we have noted before—the Bible promises a special spurning.

What Jerry wishes Peter to know about, to believe exists outside of literature, is this world of the West Side rooming house with its miserable denizens making their demands, and represented in their grossest form by the landlady and her dog. Twin guardians of its entrance, "the gatekeepers of my dwelling" as Jerry puts it, they are both "garbage", eaters of garbage—the most extreme representations of the animal existence's dual extremes of behaviour, lust and murderous rage (pp. 33-4, 38). Thus their demands—that is, the necessity of Jerry's accommodating himself to their joint natures—are the severest testing of his own withdrawal from human contact, his own isolation of spirit. They are his personal obstacle-course, and in his way Jerry has learned how to pass the test—by finding within himself that which they represent, that which he must acknowledge in himself. This is his message to Peter.

But Peter will not hear. And so, because of Jerry's previously stated and now repeated discovery of the need for the use of indirect means to solve certain problems (p. 36), it becomes necessary to take another approach: the same used by Jesus when he met with an audience too unsophisticated or too corrupted to respond—a parable. Jerry begins portentously, quite conscious of the way his choice of deliberately theatrical means of telling his story gives it a greater dramatic impact and more possibility of its being understood; by this means of "THE STORY OF JERRY AND THE DOG" Albee the dramatist shifts his play into an epic mode from its earlier apparently naturalistic but actually expressionist one.[2] Throughout the length of this narration (pp. 36-44) the first mode is suspended, to be resumed later, bringing with it the crucial question: Will Peter understand?

Jerry's Sermon on the Mount in Central Park closely allies loving and the act of prayer; for having poisoned the "monster" of black lust and rage, Jerry finds himself telling of the beast's recovery with mock-Biblical awe:

> . . . AND IT CAME TO PASS THAT THE BEAST WAS DEATHLY ILL. I knew this because he no longer attended me, and because the landlady sobered up. She stopped me in the hall the same evening of the attempted murder and confided the information that God had struck her puppy-dog a surely fatal blow. She had forgotten her bewildered lust, and her eyes were wide open for the first time. They looked like the dog's eyes. She snivelled and implored me to pray for the animal. I wanted to say to her: Madam, I have myself to pray for, the colored queen, the Puerto Rican family, the person in the front room whom I've never seen, the woman who cries deliberately behind her closed door, and the rest of the people in all roominghouses, everywhere; besides, Madam, I don't understand how to pray . . .
>
> (p. 40)

But unless the animal to which he has given poisoned hamburger be "a descendant of the puppy that guarded the gates of hell", Jerry admits as a possibility (p. 40), there

152

remains the fact of the beast's recovery—with nothing to account for it but Jerry's new desire to have the dog return to health so that he might have the chance to see what their "new relationship" would come to. And indeed Jerry now loves the dog; violence and love alone had each failed, but the combination proved powerful (p. 42). Peculiar are the ways in which love seeks its object—knows it and attempts to possess it. It is a gospel of love with an exceptional twist.

The source of this twist was undoubtedly Carson McCullers, whose *novella* "The Ballad of the Sad Cafe" Albee later turned into a play.[3] McCullers' famous story, "A Tree. A Rock. A Cloud", resembles the present Albee play in structure and theme; essentially a long harangue by a strange travelling man to a young boy, it makes only token attempts to break up what is primarily an essay by using such methods of fiction as action, description, and dialogue. McCullers' doctrine resembles what Albee's Jerry now begins to tell of: the idea that human beings are so difficult to love, so remote of access, that a candidate-lover ought to warm up, as it were, by first trying to relate to less-than-human things (hence the story's title), then work one's way up the ladder of creation to the human Other. The price of what McCullers' character calls a "science" appears to be a lengthy loneliness, its rewards the warmth of indiscriminate loving. Albee's vision is bleaker, its world of possibility tawdrier, its necessities more tragic. But it also contains more love-referents, the possibilities of relating to "a strongbox . . . WITHOUT A LOCK" and "with God" (p. 42). What Jerry has learned is that

> neither kindness nor cruelty by themselves, independent of each other, creates any effect beyond themselves; and I have learned that the two combined, together, at the same time, are the teaching emotion. And what is gained is loss . . .
>
> (p. 44)

For what is the point of having a word of love if the price is perpetual misunderstanding, Jerry asks (p. 44).

But as Peter loudly proclaims, "I DON'T UNDERSTAND!" (p. 45), Jerry's options lessen. When he tries to tickle Peter into attention (pp. 47-8), he realizes that nothing short of direct action can reach another person; speech has failed, almost as though Peter were another version of the dog, the landlady. And as with the dog, violent interaction is the only alternative. Therefore, Jerry tells Peter something of what he has discovered at the zoo, all the time pushing Peter over on his own bench; his words about trying to find out "the way people exist with animals, and the way animals exist with each other, and with people too" (p. 49) are largely ignored, but the territorial threat to Peter's bench he represents (pp. 49-59) provides the play with the remainder of its action. In contrast with the word-encapsulated offstage action just concluded, Albee's dramatic shift has undeniable power, more than if the same events had been conventionally introduced. Words now assist action, rather than taking primacy of place: Jerry insults Peter with the term "vegetable", which in Jerry's idiom implies a failure to pass the savagery test; "JESUS, you make me sick", he taunts him (p. 53). And the insult is answered in kind: "God da . . . mn you" (p. 53). There is no help for Peter, for the cops are all over on the other side of the park "chasing fairies down from the trees or out of the bushes", and Peter doesn't need this bench, having his own "little zoo" at home (pp. 54-5). He must face Jerry's angry question, arguably the core query of this entire play: "Stupid! Don't you have any idea, not even the slightest, what other people *need?*" (p. 56).

Thus it is by offering Peter first the verbal possibility that he may be a bit of a man after all, and then by throwing down in front of him an opened knife, that Jerry sets up the final dramatic gesture of the play: his own impalement, to which he adds the words (so reminiscent of Christ's crucifixion) "So be it!" (pp. 57-9). This doubled consummation becomes what Albee's directions call a "tableau", for once again the dramatic underpinnings have been radically altered. Reference has been made to the play having a sonata structure. It would be even more accurate to call the final three pages of text a coda, different in quality from what has gone before. For this matter is highly symbolic and ritualized, its stage depiction balletic, even mimetic. Peter screams, as does Jerry: "the sound of an infuriated and fatally wounded animal" (p. 59). And now Peter is ready, as he calls out repeatedly "Oh my God!" in what is less a plea than a symbolic recognition, for Jerry's acknowledgement of his sharing in animal nature (pp. 60-1). Jerry's enemy is "indifference", a trait he has long since begun to suspect God of (p. 43); we might profitably compare, for example, Osborne's *Look Back in Anger*. Now Jerry's language is contrivedly, but justifiably, Biblical in tone and import: "I came unto you . . . and you have comforted me. Dear Peter" (p. 61). And Jerry now can acknowledge that Peter has managed to qualify as "an animal" at last, if barely. At the end, when Jerry picks up Peter's call to God, it is—as the stage directions tell us—with "a combination of scornful mimicry and supplication" (p. 62).

Peter's offstage "OH MY GOD!" (p. 62), when it is quietly repeated by the dying Jerry as the play's final line, is the ultimate testimonial to the power of Jerry's epiphany working through a second party. The God, the Beloved, within each of us can be recognized only within the flash of lightning. Albee's play about the need to keep an animal within us alive is also a *tour-de-force* of dramatic styles and methods. In its short space of action and language, it manages to make a theoretically unlikely combination of ingredients work, and work exceedingly well. The play continues to shock even those who cannot "understand" it, which is to say that its structure accomplishes on its audience what its parable and knife-dance do for Peter: they make him see the animal within; they make him play the man. Or so we hope, for the play does not forecast the future state-of-soul of its second lead, now that his crash course in Love (by means of parable and demonstration) is ended. One can only hope that his denial days are over, and his apostleship begun.

NOTES

1 Edward Albee, *The Zoo Story*, in *Three Plays* (New York, 1960). All pages references appear parenthetically within my text.
2 It is interesting to observe that in Edward Albee's own 1979 production of this play, the naturalistic took far greater precedence over the expressionistic than one might have expected. Indeed, some of the key lines in this interpretation would appear to have been either cut or de-emphasized. Quite likely Albee has decided, in the two decades which have intervened, that his original writing was far too explicitly "clear" to

be sustained. At any rate, the recent impositions seem to have been ordered in the interests of dramatic subtlety: the single bench; the method acting.

3 Carson McCullers, "A Tree. A Rock. A Cloud", in *The Ballad of the Sad Cafe: The Novels and Stories of Carson McCullers* (Boston, 1951), pp. 131-39, esp. 138.

12

Arden's Eucharistic Christ: *Serjeant Musgrave's Dance*

In his best-known play, *Serjeant Musgrave's Dance* (1959),[1] John Arden provides us with a vision of a Christ fragmented and distributed among a congregation of the distressed and the bewildered. Though it touches rather simplistically on issues of power and its exercise, the play deals movingly and genuinely with the theme of redemptive love as anodyne for the evils of rampant intellectuality, whether of the public or the private variety. Such love, where and when it appears, must necessarily be partial, inadequate, and doomed to temporary defeats: in other words, be human. Opposed to it are values which of their very natures are sterile, unloving, and prone to abuse—in short, non-human. Indeed, the latter may be called satanic by reason of their assumption of divine perogatives by lesser, however "angelic", intelligences. *Serjeant Musgrave's Dance* pits the values of the Old Testament, with its emphasis upon a strict and retributive justice, squarely against those of the New, with its gospel of love, forgiveness, and mercy.

In Arden's scheme of things, the central, but rather forbiddingly frigid, figure of Serjeant Musgrave himself is explicitly attached to an antique vision of a judging God the Father, whereas love and mercy are distributed as attributes among a variety of persons, most notably the women characters, but also among Musgrave's followers—disciples, or "sons" as they may be called. Thus a theme of regeneration is a substantial part of the drama: what the past, the Father, makes necessary, or imposes upon humankind through sheer force of will and mind, the future is able to redeem through passion and suffering, but especially through acceptance of the rule of Love. It is "Black Jack" Musgrave's play, and the absolutes in which his rigid mind conceives the world to exist are reinforced by the play's stark dependence upon a colour dichotomy of red and black. Black may stand for evil, for the hard matter—coal—by which the colliers earn their living, for death, or for anarchy; red may mean love, blood, the uniforms of soldiers, or a benign socialism. Despite the ironic interrelationship of these associations, however, the colours black and red become for Serjeant Musgrave the sharp alternatives of some perfectible, theoretically Hegelian world—a deluded system of opposed values as simplistic as a deck of cards. Musgrave's Messiahship, which has made with-me-or-against-me the core of Christ's mission, is ultimately as death-centred as what it seeks to supplant.

Arden reinforces the rigour of his pseudo-dialectic with further elements of deliberate theatricality. His play opens with a game of cards in progress, a "play" within a play. After the first lines of speech, Sparky sings the first of the several songs the play contains. It is a soldier's lament over his recruitment, and it is thus ironically pertinent to the recruiting mission of just these characters; also establishes the note of offhand rancour, of angry·resignation undercut by black humour, that permeates the play. The simultaneous action of the card game creates the suggestion that what is to follow is also a game, and thus of slight importance. Still, both song and card game are, arguably, epic-theatre devices that objectify the issues to be presented, making dispassionate consideration possible, according to Brechtian theory. In the world of Jack Musgrave's mind, we are meant to note the symbolic potential of such ostensibly naturalistic speeches as this:

> ATTERCLIFFE: . . . The black spades carry the day. Jack, King and Ace. *We* throw the red Queen over . . .
>
> (p. 9)

We are only lines away from the first meeting of Black Jack Musgrave (p. 10), but already colour symbolism has been introduced for our remembrance, and with it a complex series of suggestions and associations crucial to the play are laid out for our perusal.

Moreover, the song mentions the central theme of victimisation, of fate (or the weight of a system) singling out persons for sacrifice. Later, this scene might be related to the casting of lots in the Passion narrative; but for now, we may note that one martyr-victim is already present (though we cannot realise it as yet), and that Arden is not letting the Biblical implications of this scene go to waste. For one thing, it is—fittingly enough for opening events—a cold winter's night on which men are shown waiting for some signal arrival; but for another, befitting the ending of things, we are also given an emphasis on death—the disappointment attending the career of the false Messiah:

> SPARKY: How much longer we got to wait, I'd like to know. I want to be off aboard that damned barge and away. What's happened to our Black Jack Musgrave, eh? Why don't he come and give us the word to get going?
>
> (p. 10)

And Sparky's song now goes on to tell of desertion, and of the deserter's betrayal by his "cruel sweetheart", followed by the deserter's death by hanging on "the high gallows tree" (p. 10). It is the story of Everyman's crucifixion, given the insufficiency of love.

The centrality of the thematic content of song and dialogue at this early point in the play is confirmed by Hurst's nervous anger upon hearing the rest of Sparky's song; calling it a "God-damned devil of a song to sing on this sort of a journey!" he "glances nervously around" as though the dead man they are accompanying could hear them (p. 10). That this dead man might be the pivot of their mission develops only over a number of pages, but already the audience is meant to feel unease at "his" presence. So the card game must continue, especially after Sparky has asked Hurst whether he is "a man and a soldier" or "an old red rag stretched over four pair o' bones" (p. 11). The card game thus takes on a quasi-naturalistic function: it replaces consideration of an unseemly real problem with a game, an excuse for non-thought. And yet it is just this sort of human response that takes the stark terror out of the rigid opposition of the forces that were discussed at the beginning of

159

this chapter. Far better to idle one's career away than to be one of Life's mistaken heroes; far better a game than the face of the devil.

In effect, the closest thing to a genuine devil in Arden's play now appears, as if on cue: the figure of the Bargee, who comes on whistling "Michael Finnegan". Through his identification with this Joycean song of perpetual rebeginnings, the Bargee comes to stand for something more than the survivorship of Robert Bolt's Common Man. Adept at instigation as well as survival, he is also on the side of trouble, but trouble of the sort that makes for no essential changes. He is a cynic as well as an aggravator—at any rate, something stronger than a mere catalyst. The Bargee likes to meddle, whatever the consequences. Clever devil, he is intelligent enough to further intensify existing antagonisms, such as those related to the colour scheme already mentioned. He reminds the soldiers that they are known as "bloodred roses" (p. 12), and that they will be encountering special enemies in a coal-mining town (pp. 13-14). Not that Musgrave, in spite of his preoccupations, does not recognise the Bargee's nature; indeed, he warns him not to bother his men (p. 13). But the Bargee, a nihilistic Švejk, simply retreats somewhat and goes on jibing. In the face of Musgrave's "curt" reminder that "A soldier's duty is a soldier's life", the Bargee raises a song of his own, on the subject of duty:

> The Empire wars are far away
> For duty's sake we sail away
> Me arms and leg is shot away
> And all for the wink of a shilling and a drink . . .
>
> (p. 14)

Scene One ends with all values in question, and nothing certain.

Scene Two opens (pp. 14-15) with a strong contrasting of clearly defined values—the Parson's lack of feeling opposed to Mrs. Hitchcock's charity and general humanity. The Parson is one of Arden's unashamedly caricatured personages; he typifies so many bad parsons in so many plays that he hardly commands any stage presence at all, except among those for whom this sort of anti-clericalism is a novelty. He can be played (given the theatre's ability to give some sort of reality to whatever it presents) convincingly enough, but cannot develop much interest and sympathy from the audience. But the charitable Mrs. Hitchcock alludes to the play's colour theme in a way that counteracts crude oppositions:

> I am a proud coalowner
> And in scarlet here I stand.
> Who shall come or who shall go
> Through all my coal-black land?

(p. 15)

Here the oppositions of red and black are seen as false, or at most as specimens of a similar reifying mentality at work.

With the Bargee's entrance, the scene's values change; the Bargee speaks to the Parson, but his dramatic function is to animate Annie, who till now has been silently polishing glasses upstage. It is Annie who responds to the Bargee's pinch with the taunt of "bloody dog", and then sings a song about the value of soldiers (pp. 17-18):

> Because we know he'll soon be dead
> We strap our arms round the scarlet red
> Then send him weeping over the sea.

(p. 18)

And Annie will not, according to her principles, sleep with all these soldiers in one night. We do not yet suspect Annie's dramatic function, but we already have an inkling of her worth; an adequate performance of the play should demonstrate her positive strength.

In comes the Major, to a mocking introduction by the Bargee "to the present" (p. 21). This is Arden's second caricature-figure; the Bargee mocks him, and the text itself hardly does him better. Again, like the Parson, he lacks feeling and principle. He reveals himself as a pragmatist (p. 22): he wishes to clear space in the town—with the help of the Queen's wars. He is in complicity with the Parson, except that the Parson is also concerned with preserving the community's external moral code: he will have none of the usual recruits' swagger and fornication—because he is "religious" (p. 24) (like the sister-in-law in Brecht's *Caucasian Chalk Circle*). Musgrave follows the Mayor's departure with a simple meal of bread and cheese—

161

not a Christ-like one, for he forswears drink, but a Puritan's abstemious snack (p. 25).

The confrontation between Musgrave and Annie, given the weight of its implications for the play as a whole, takes on the tone of Mary Magdalen's first meeting with Christ; yet its values are intentionally opposite. Bringing him bread and cheese, she describes him instantly, and accurately enough:

> The North Wind in a pair of millstones
> Was your father and your mother
> They got you in a cold grinding.
> God help us all if they get you a brother.

(p. 26)

Musgrave acknowledges the essential rightness of what Annie has said, and speaks of it to Mrs. Hitchcock, who has already astonished the gathering with a riddle of her own (p. 20). And just as naturally, he shifts the subject to the dead Billy Hicks, for he has an appropriate audience. And Mrs. Hitchcock remembers that Billy would come there, "pissed of a Sat'dy night", and sing religious hymns, and that he gave Annie a baby, a sickly one that died within two months (pp. 26-7). Indeed, the child and its father died more or less together. But, Musgrave speculates, "Dead men and dead children should bide where they're put and not be rose up to the thoughts of the living" (p. 27). Yet it is just such a resurrection, a violent irruption into the lives of the yet-living, that Black Jack Musgrave has in mind. But father and child, resurrected, are intended to bring with them a message of death, not of life, and to provide no comfort to the mother and lover they left behind. And as if to confirm his false and mechanical Christness, Musgrave sends his men and himself to the four ways out of town to scout for intelligence (himself to the north, because he has heard it suits his nature), to rendezvous later at the churchyard, the abode of death (p. 27).

In the third scene, which now follows, it becomes apparent that the soldiers have become pariahs in the eyes of the townspeople, especially the striking colliers (pp. 27-8). As Musgrave arrives, complaining of the place's coldness, each of his men reports hostility in the town, each man ritually beginning his report with "Hardly a thing. Street empty, . . ." (pp. 28-9). This

ARDEN'S EUCHARISTIC CHRIST

ritual of threes complements the scene's eerie menace, but does not seem meant to suggest any religious significance. It is Hurst who notes that the soldiers are "on the run" in red uniforms in a cold setting of black and white (p. 29). In the midst of these stark and Puritanical oppositions, Musgrave at last speaks directly of his sense of mission; he, who has already certified his belief in the soldier's commitment to duty, begins to define exactly what he means by the "word" by which he lives:

> . . . because my power's the power of God, and that's what's brought me here and all three of you with me. You know my words and purposes . . .
>
> (p. 30)

And he chides the nervous Hurst, who says he does not believe in God and also says that their mission is to inform the people of how Billy Hicks died so that there will be no more wars, by emphasizing the divinity of just that mission:

> Which *is* the word of God! Our message without God is a bad belch and a hiccup. You three of you, without me, are a bad belch and a hiccup . . .
>
> (p. 31)

But the lecture on God a-coming is briefly interrupted.

Even before the entrance of the colliers, the issues between Musgrave and Hurst have been laid out; the latter is a classic political libertarian, his morality based upon humanitarian concerns, but he is also, at this point in the play, incapable of independent action. Arden has created a character whose defects, at least initially, retard the rhetorical efficacy of his thinking. Because Hurst is "alone, stupid, without a gill of discipline, illiterate, ignorant of the Scriptures" (p. 31), he is required to accept authority from Musgrave, and join *his* Cromwellian campaign. For throughout much of the play, Musgrave appears to have affairs under his control; for instance, he quiets the angry colliers in this scene, with nice political sidestepping. Indeed, one of the colliers pays Musgrave the tribute of calling him "Johnny Clever" (p. 33). With the colliers gone again, Musgrave is free to continue his harangue: to spell out the nature and purpose of their mission as he, uniquely, conceives of it.

Attercliffe is opposed to all wars, wars in general, as "sin",
but Musgrave seems obsessed, or maddened, by the aftermath
of the death of Billy Hicks and the need to make appropriate
expiation for it: "We've come to this town to work the guilt back
to where it began" (pp. 33-4). It is to bring the news of Billy's
death back to the town where he was born that the men have
come here, as Sparky recites the matter in a trembling voice
(pp. 34-5). But what the others may conceive of as a mission to
preach against wars, especially colonial ones, Sparky makes a
personal matter (it was *his* "dead mucker" they have brought
along with them); while Musgrave considers it a business so
generalized that only a God may hold it entire within his
imagination. There then follows an unusual recurrence of the
name "God" within the play: Sparky taunts the other men with
being so distant from Billy that to them he is "like God";
Musgrave picks up the pieces of the dispute in order to inform
them all that, thanks to him, the men have "discipline",
"grief", "good order", and that all of these have been "turned
to the works of God!" (p. 35). God is first the most distant of
agencies, next the focus of all their efforts, and shortly he is to
appear among them.

Musgrave now begins his disquisition on "the Word". First
he reminds the men that they have been given a special
opportunity to work their changes in the town:

> . . . The winter's giving us one day, two days, three days even—
> that's clear safe for us to hold our time, take count of the
> corruption, then stand before this people with our white shining
> word, and let it dance! It's a hot coal, this town, despite that it's
> freezing—choose your minute and blow: and whoosh, she's
> flamed your roof off!
>
> (pp. 35-6)

In Musgrave's fanatic vision, then, the distinctions of image
and colour with which we began are to be replaced by a new
meaning, the released energy of the dancing Word:

> MUSGRAVE *(with angry articulation)*: We are here with a word.
> That's all. That's particular. Let the word dance. That's all
> that's material, this day and for the next. What happens
> afterwards, the Lord God will provide. I am with you, He said.
> Abide with Me in Power. A Pillar of Flame before the people.

164

What we show here'll lead forward forever, against dishonour, and greed, and murder-for-greed! There is our duty, the new, deserter's duty: God's dance on this earth: and all that we are is His four strong legs to dance it . . .

(p. 36)

But the nature of the Word and the Deed is not yet defined, at least not for the men. As they file out obediently, Musgrave poses himself in a soliloquy of Shakespearean proportions. The trouble is that the Bargee is also there, mocking his speech; in it, the Serjeant addresses his God directly, confessing himself His agent and admitting that his mind had become muddled by warfare, but now would be, if God would keep his mind clear, a fulfiller of new duties, one who would "change all soldiers' duties":

. . . My prayer is: keep my mind clear so I can weigh Judgement against the Mercy and Judgement against the Blood, and make this Dance as terrible as You have put it into my brain. The Word alone is terrible: the Deed must be worse. But I know it is Your Logic, and You will provide.

(p. 37)

It is a frightening speech, filled with glimpses of horrors yet to come; and it is worth considering from a theatrical standpoint, for an understanding of its dramatic function as conclusion to Act I is necessary to the appreciation of the progress of the entire play.

In terms of language, Arden has elevated his sights in this closing speech: vague references to forthcoming action have become contained in "the Word"; and now that the Word is being described as a "Dance", theatricality itself presents the shift in values from observed action to significant speech, to transcendent and formalized movement, and to balletic ritual. The Dance will be parody-Christian by being Dionysiac, by letting loose the lower energies upon the stage in a destructive ecstasy. It is to be, of course, a Dance of Death, but it is something more. As has been suggested, the dance motif is emphasized by being picked up at the start of Act II, where the drunken colliers dance to the urgings-on of the Bargee (pp. 38-41). Yet this literal dancing has been foreshadowed by Musgrave's speech at the end of Act I. Musgrave intends it not

165

so much as a soliloquy as a prayer, a dialogue with God in which God's lines are, in effect, also "heard"; and the dramatic effect of the scene is undercut and altered drastically by the Bargee's mockery. The Bargee's function in the scene, in other words, is to throw its contents into ironic relief, and at least to deny the Dance an unequivocal sense and purpose. If Musgrave wants to play the Messiah, this is a Gethsemane scene with a mocking imp visible in the background.

The colliers' dance is accompanied by the Bargee's playing a mouth-organ and by Sparky's drumming; some moments later, it is the drum-rolls that silence the crowd that gathers to hear Musgrave's pronouncements. The Bargee's mockery of Musgrave, already apparent to the audience, is nearly sensed by Musgrave himself; and yet there is one point (p. 41) at which the Bargee makes the mistake of dancing clumsily to his own tune, and when, by identifying his regiment with Annie, he nearly makes his position all too clear:

> BARGEE: I'll tell you, me lovely, why not? The Queen's Own Randy Chancers: or the Royal Facing-Both-Ways—hey, me clever monkeys:
> Old Joe looks out for Joe
> Plots and plans and who lies low?
> But the Lord provides, says Crooked Old Joe.

Musgrave becomes briefly suspicious, but the Bargee excuses his remark and song as a joke, and makes a hurried exit—at which the crowd, deprived of its instigator, quietens somewhat. We should remember that the substance of the songs which we hear during this scene is the relationship between war and love, personified, of course, in the soldiers and their girls.

Thus it is in contrast to this cynicism about the existing society that the pairing of Hurst and Annie takes place. We are told that she watches him as he complains to Musgrave about the insufficiency of the Word (p. 43), and his clear appeal to this girl who has already been hurt because she has trusted soldiers must be judged with reference to the opposition of his character to Musgrave's. Thereafter, her approach to him is clear and direct (pp. 44-5), but their encounter is interrupted by the Bargee's bringing in the Constable to shut the bar down. Given the Bargee's presence and the general atmosphere of jealousy about men and uniform and women, it is not surprising that a near-murder takes place, deeply shocking Attercliffe, who leaves for the company of the dead Billy Hicks (pp. 47-9). But with the Bargee, that self-confessed opportunist, absent, complicity develops between Annie and the three soldiers— each of them acting out a version of humane concern over the issues of the play—which is shortly to become vividly evident onstage, and which in its clarity delineates Arden's handling of the theme of the fragmented or Eucharistic Christ. That is, we are being readied for a distribution of the play's Christ-presence.

The final moments of the first scene of Act II involve a confrontation between Musgrave and Annie, bringing to a head the issues between them and what they respectively stand for in the play. Musgrave specifically associates Annie with the political state of "anarchy", as opposed to his own sense of duty: his "plan":

> . . . But if you come to us with what you call your life or love—*I'd* call it your indulgence—and you scribble all over that plan, you make it crooked, dirty, idle, untidy, *bad*—there's anarchy.
>
> (p. 51)

Musgrave's revelations of his compulsions towards order are the definitions of his shortcomings, and they give Annie a sense of her own emergent power; we are told that she now smiles for the first time in the play. Even if we do not recognize this smile as that of a personified and beatific Love, we must note that Annie has now joined with Musgrave's own men in anarchic combat against their superior.

We next see the Bargee drilling the colliers, a parody of the order Musgrave stands for. One man, Walsh, has enough individuality to warrant possession of a surname; he invokes the name of God quite often, though he rejects what he takes to be Musgrave's commitment to a passive Christ of a maintained system:

> Gentle Jesus send us rest
> Surely the bosses knows what's best!
>
> (p. 54)

This brief scene ends with the Bargee, who is whistling his tune

167

of immutability, forming a queer compact with Walsh—in the name of a "proper" kind of "riot" (p. 56). Here Arden has managed to define and oppose the forces of war and of love.

Act III, Scene 2 is Arden's nearest approach to expressionist stagecraft in this play. Musgrave in his bedroom dominates the stage, yet his downstage men in their stable stalls are closer to the audience in physical position, as well as sympathies. "God's awake", says Sparky of Musgrave, whose light is still on. The joke becomes somewhat less fanciful when Annie arrives at Hurst's box just as Musgrave puts that light out for sleep (pp. 57-8). Her advances to Hurst are resisted in Musgrave's name, whereupon Annie exclaims "My Christ" and "Christ, let me stay with you", reminding Hurst that Musgrave called her "life and love" (pp. 59-60). Attercliffe would welcome her but for his sense of guilt (pp. 60-1). So Sparky is left; he tells Annie that Hurst is already like God, whom he identifies as Musgrave. Sparky fears madness, and during his speeches Musgrave recalls the killing of civilians (pp. 62-3). All of this leads to Annie's remembering her Sparky-like lover, who left her with "a twisted little thing dead" that resembled a "little withered clover—three in one it made" (p. 63). Annie's dead baby, a parody of conventional visualisations of the Trinity, sounds like the embodiment of the anarchy Musgrave described earlier. "Bad shape. Dead" she calls it, rousing Sparky's sympathy for her, and also his passion—upon which Musgrave screams in his sleep about the burning of London, the deaths of the civilians, and the end of the world (p. 64). Musgrave is seen, upstage, as a God in agony (Annie calls him that), while downstage the temporary lovers try to forget the rigours of duty and its deadly results (pp. 64-5). Sparky rejects the role of being one of Musgrave's "angels", hoping to escape with Annie; but the loyalist Hurst rushes in, there is a ludicrous tussle over Sparky's trousers, and in the ensuing melee Sparky is killed, falling on a bayonet held, without malice, by Attercliffe—who exclaims "O Holy God!" at this demonstration of guilt's inexorable contagion (p. 68). Musgrave is back in power, for the forces of love are disorganised, and cannot act.

Mrs. Hitchcock and Annie are both terribly confused by what has happened: the former mutters about "the end of the world" (Musgrave's phrase) and promises to lock Annie away, as Musgrave asks, for "It may be the best thing. I've got to trust you, haven't I? I've always praised religion" (p. 70). In this way Arden shows the principle of order establishing its rule in the world because of the vacuum of power in human affairs. Rejecting Attercliffe's claims that Sparky's death cancels out old debts (p. 73), Musgrave saves Walsh from the effects of the treason of his erstwhile ally, the Bargee, and proceeds with his own plans in the guise of staging a recruiting rally. Thus the Act ends with apparent confusion everywhere, with the national colours prominently displayed, while in actuality the figure of order—Musgrave—looms over all, seemingly well in control.

The way is thus prepared for the lengthy first scene of the final act; the market-place is ready for its rally, with the Bargee now acting towards the audience as he has hitherto acted towards other characters. His mocking song (p. 77) is justified when the Parson clearly and contemptibly misuses the Christian gospel to further the aims of empire, anachronistically calling for violence on behalf of "the responsibilities of a first-class power" (p. 79). And just as anachronistic is Musgrave's subsequent description of Army life (p. 81); all this is accomplished while Musgrave is, as we have noted, in apparent power. (In reality, it can be claimed, the Bargee and his sort have control.) But Musgrave and his surviving men now put forth the claims of duty, though clearly in mutual conflict (pp. 82-4); they promise to display Duty's flag, and do: the "articulated skeleton" of Billy Hicks (p. 84). At last, Musgrave sings and dances quite literally, reminding the townspeople that Billy is the thing they cannot evade or forget (pp. 84-5). Pages of delayed exposition follow, along with clear statements from Musgrave rejecting any arguments that attack his sense of duty; and when Walsh seems to think the matter amounts to a simple rejection of recruitment (as against staying and supporting the strike effort), Musgrave introduces the skeleton itself as the town's very own Billy. The Serjeant calls himself "religious", and seeks to establish the hand of God in this: that is, he seeks to lay the blame for Billy's death to a system that made it inevitable that someone like Billy would die. "There used to by my duty: now there's a disease", he continues; he and his friends are there because the townsfolk have rejected "Moses and the Prophets" and therefore—as

169

Christ reminded his hearers[2]—there would have to be a stronger lesson given (p. 90). Here is Musgrave's scriptural basis for playing the Christ; indeed, even Walsh acknowledges it, sarcastically, in his reference to "your little gospel" (p. 91).

But Walsh also rejects that gospel—refuses to kill the ones who cause the killing, even though Musgrave has selected him as a like-minded disciple (p. 92). Attercliffe also deserts; only Hurst, perhaps, will stand by Musgrave on the principle of preventive murder (pp. 93-4). But there are dragoons on the road, and Annie has appeared to remind the crowd of the dead Sparky; and when Hurst would fire the Gatling gun, it is Attercliffe—arms out, Christlike—who stands in front of the muzzle (p. 96). When Musgrave and Hurst quarrel over logic, the latter deserts just in time to be cut down by the arriving dragoons (pp. 96-7). Ironic cries of "Saved!" greet the dragoons (p. 97), and when Walsh wonders what to do now, the Bargee answers:

> Free beer. It's still here.
> No more thinking. Easy drinking.
> End of a bad bad dream. Gush forth the foaming stream.
>
> (p. 99)

Having just changed sides again, this man who has just been haranguing us, the audience, advises resumption of the old familiar round, which seems to be the meaning of the final Dance. But not everybody dances. For one, Annie sits, *Pietà*-like, with the skeleton of her dead lover over her knees; for another, though Walsh joins the Bargee in the Dance, Musgrave and Attercliffe of course do not (pp. 99-100).

All of which is answered, if arbitrarily, in the final scene. Indeed, Mrs. Hitchcock refers to this process as gleaning "the moral" (p. 101); she is allowed Arden's alliterative triumph, calling Musgrave a "gormless great gawk!" (p. 101). Thus she rams his logic down his throat: there must be an end to retribution, and to attempt to "cure the pox by further whoring" (p. 102). Musgrave is silenced; it is left to Attercliffe to sing the final song, one in which a hope of new beginnings is held forth—one, curiously enough, dependent upon the image of the Tree:

For the apple holds a seed will grow
In live and lengthy joy
To raise a flourishing tree of fruit
For ever and a day.

(p. 104)

Thus, though both men are about to be raised to death upon a tree—crucified, in effect—there is yet the hope of change. *Serjeant Musgrave's Dance* ends with this hopefulness, the vision of a tree of death that yet may be a tree of life.

By dividing its Christ-presence into three, or four, *Serjeant Musgrave's Dance* replies to the violent misuse of power in the world, quite clearly replacing an Ibsenian God of Duty and a Shavian God of Power with truly Christian substitutes. Women, as is theatrically traditional, stand for love, and give of it freely; men have the task of putting love into action. That burden falls upon the Sons of "God" in this play, each of them responding, with various degrees of commitment, along a spectrum running from Duty to Love. Given mankind's general predicament, its natural complicity in its own disasters, whatever hope exists seems to spring from the human willingness to choose death rather than submit to institutional regimentation. This is a play about a false Messiah, a man who really aspired to the role of God the Father, and thus resembled Lucifer. In his wake are those lesser mortals, the members of a fragmented humanity, who choose the path of love. They are mankind's real Christs, their way a real Passion.

NOTES

1 John Arden, *Serjeant Musgrave's Dance* (London, 1960). All page references appear parenthetically within my text.
2 See Luke 16:19-31, especially 16:31, the story of the rich man and the beggar Lazarus. As Eliot's Prufrock knows, and as some of the other plays considered in this volume agree, some people would not even believe a Lazarus risen from the dead. Musgrave's apparent threat is to let the dead Billy "speak", in effect, with the implicit further promise of the fires of hell—as in the Bible text. Yet the Biblical Christ would seem to suggest, and by his own endeavour, that there is always a chance for another ordinary person to give—by means of his own death, his own rising again—witness to the rule of love. By "ordinary", of course, we understand a universal imminence of the Christ-pattern: the dramatist's possible Everyman.

13

Whiting's Self-Possessed: *The Devils*

One might almost imagine John Whiting himself creating the pun on self-possession with which this consideration of his play *The Devils* (1960-61)[1] will begin, for its central idea is the relationship between apparent possession by devils from without and the tragic implications of attempting to acknowledge fully the demands of human nature—possession, that is, from within. Whiting's acute verbal inventiveness suggests that the possible pun would not escape him. It is especially interesting, moreover, to regard *The Devils* as a late manifestation of an approach to character that is found in such writers as Eliot and Shaw, and to examine Whiting's thoughts on the Christ-figure in the light of earlier attainments and commitments. Above all, however, the play itself has great impact as drama, its material so rich that no warping is required to make it fit the thematic frame that is proposed for it here.

We need not be concerned with the particular historical event, the mass-possession in Loudon, which attracted artists as varied as Aldous Huxley and Krzysztof Penderecki; what matters is why the case particularly appealed to John Whiting, who had never before tackled such an inherently melodramatic subject. Not wishing to argue with the relatively small number of Whiting scholars and critics, it could be suggested that his vision of human predicament found itself conveniently projected upon the historical facts of the Loudon possession case, and that the resolution of that case could contain the germ of Whiting's notions of the lessons of history. As is hardly surprising in such situations, the establishment of such a convenient mutuality of statement requires the presence of a tragic figure, a sacrificial personage, or both. The priest Grandier goes a long way towards satisfying both requisites.

As a noun, the name Grandier suggests a pride-bearing tree. When Jeanne growls the name out, it might imply, Give us, O Lord, the thing we cannot live without—which, in this case, is sexual intercourse. The pathos of *The Devils* is achieved by its puritanical abstinence; its intended lovers do not meet until, their fates assured by the separate and yet interlinked operation of their roles and natures, they are mutually condemned. In a better world, we are meant to think, such things would not occur. Repression would give way to signal victory, and like would find its like.

Not so in *The Devils*. The persecution and death of Grandier are but the ritual taunting of society's scapegoat; he is killed not only for certain temporary benefit, but also because that is what society requires. The Dionysiac panting of Whiting's style is the direct result of the ritualistic fervour it seeks to depict. We need to kill the thing we might become: Urbain Grandier. We have not yet become this combination of the worldly and the proud that his name suggests he is. Ours is an existence that combines the prideful with the need to subjugate, the wish to build together with the need to stand abashed. Grandier threatens to escape this deadening duality; he must be destroyed, therefore. This dramatic purpose is abetted by the characterization of Grandier as paralleled by the consistent presentation of humanity as naturally depraved.

We should not, therefore, be surprised to find—with hindsight—that the first scene is dominated by such figures as Adam and Mannoury. They are survivors—dispassionate, and intellectually interested in seeing justice served. Insofar as they are apt to instigate or aggravate situations that result in pain or disorder, however, they are akin to Arden's meddling Bargee. We see them first beneath a gallows, speaking of Grandier, and shortly to wonder what survives of a man who is slain. Phillipe passes by, the corpse causing her to state her preference for sensual thoughts—the way her legs move in dancing, for example. If disinterested inquiry is revealed, all too often, as being a metamorphosis of cruelty, we may note in this juxtaposition of character types that innocence, the presumed opposite of a jaded knowing-all, has its own proximity to death. Phillipe's thoughts may be superficially directed to heaven, but her human longings are all too evident; Grandier's entrance provides just the dramatic element that is lacking: erotic satisfaction hedged about with moral confines. We are shown the play's polarities here, pure physicality and physical purity, and are ready for the submission of new evidence (pp. 141-42).

That evidence—indeed, the court of inquiry itself—is the person of Grandier. Whiting has his dramatic entrance, for which the audience has already been intellectually (thematically) and physically (visually) prepared by what they have seen and heard, ironically "spoiled" by Grandier's having his gown spoiled with filth thrown from the Sewerman's bucket (p. 143). Though Grandier is not disconcerted, the event has meaning central to Whiting's aims: human pride has been confronted with human excrement; sin and sinfulness—to hear the Sewerman describe his occupational milieu—are brought before the ambitious human nature from which they spring. Whiting is not about to let his audience forget for a moment the realities of their actions. It is significant that Grandier and the Sewerman get along together so well and understand each other so, for the latter is neither a Boltish Common Man nor a Shakespearean Gravedigger—though he is closer to the *Hamlet* character than to the one in *A Man for All Seasons*. He is present in order to philosophise about humanity's rootedness in mire, its inescapable connection with every sort of dirt and filth. According to the Sewerman, Grandier is not a "man", being a priest; but he does not yet truly know his interlocutor. Grandier helps him learn, speaking of his sympathy for the executed corpse that hangs nearby, a man who had stolen in order to decorate his beloved's body with gold. But the gold looked "colourless, valueless, against her golden skin. That was repentance" (p. 144). There is no mockery here, simply an acceptance of motives and an understanding of the disappointment of dreams. This, we gather, is no ordinary priest, and certainly not one with his gaze steadily fixed upon the spiritual.

Grandier is both priest and sensualist, a conflicting

combination noted by De Cerisay and D'Armagnac in the next short scene (pp. 144-45). What, they ask, will this dilemma of character lead to? But we have already seen Grandier's end foreshadowed; the hanged man with whom Grandier has sympathised is merely a type of the same inability to reconcile conflicting forces within the individual, and much closer than Grandier to being a representation of the crucified Christ. We might wonder here whether it will make sense to call Grandier a Christ, or even a martyr. Does doing so not thereby dignify the deservedly low, and demean the high? But martyrs can die for any cause, and a Christ-figure be not a whit conventionally divine, if playwrights wish them so. Grandier represents a spirit which, to Whiting, is worth a death. He will suffer and die that death, and he will, in a sense, rise again. He is just what a martyr is, the Greek source of the word meaning witness, and as the other characters so far considered have also been. His witness is to the necessity of love, and he knows—he says this to Ninon, with only a trace of irony—that an act of dying, or any act, can be an act of love (p. 146). And such is his death to be.

Yet Grandier also frets over his human dilemma, his being forced together as an amalgam of body and spirit when he would wish to be something more—"Or less" (p. 146). Adam and Mannoury share his interest in this problem, but their concern is academic, sterile, dispassionate, and frigid, leading to death; being purely material, it has not spirit in it, no passion. Theirs is a scientific and amoral inquisitiveness, and Grandier is right, though unwise, to taunt them for it (pp. 146-49). But Grandier has a weakness of his own: a sensualist, he is also torn by a "ravaged humility of spirit" that makes him pray, privately, for a release from the promptings of the flesh, which have thus far accompanied the workings of his pride (p. 149). He can therefore be said to possess a certain moral breadth and depth unknown to the other characters in the play, and to be, in such a sense, Whiting's image of the questioning man of this or any other time. If there is a structural weakness to The Devils, it may stem from a lack of genuine character development: Grandier is essentially already the man he will be at the moment of his death; yet awareness of the extent of his pride has already caused him self-doubts that will bring him, in time, close to despair. Ironically, the author brings him back in the

175

end to roughly the point at which he began—an integral human being, a bundle of glorious but contradictory impulses and attainments.

It is this duality in human nature that fascinates Whiting—the urge to climb coupled with a desire to burrow in the muck. But what has a human being to rely upon, finally, but his selfhood? The enemies of human nature would ask him to deny that self as the first step in his subordination to non-self:

> DE LA ROCHEPOZAY: . . . For all vanities are an assertion of self, and the assertion of self in Man is the ascendancy of the Devil . . .
>
> (p. 150)

Whiting apparently thinks otherwise: human progress is a lengthy movement towards reliance upon our own given natures. Barré, the exorcist of devils, is made to appear rather like Robert Bolt's seller of indulgences; and yet Whiting does not dismiss the idea of possession as such, but rather gives it the dignity of unironic and accepting stage directions. The reasons may be found in Whiting's views of human nature: in the repression of its "baser" demands, the infection of "devils" begins, like worms springing from a putrefying corpse. Jeanne's devils are as real as her desires for Grandier.

There are subtle variations between Whiting's approach to possession and that of Arthur Miller in *The Crucible*, where the pretence of possession is more consciously and maliciously arrived at out of a patent jealousy, but where the issues involved are rather similar. In neither case is the theological phenomenon of possession simply accepted; in both, it is given psychological grounding. The characterisation of Barré, which now begins (pp. 150-52), is the clearest clue to Whiting's convictions. But just as relentless, though far more intelligently pursued, is the womanising of Grandier, who is next seen arranging to become the tutor of Phillipe, thereby fitting her into his busy schedule (pp. 152-53). His enemies are watching, for "lust must have a partner" (p. 154), one for whom he will deliver himself up to them. The search for physical love and the attendance of devils, then, are inextricably linked throughout this play.

As instantly as Brecht provides an Azdak for the needs of his

Grusha, Whiting dramatizes the answer to his theatrical demand, Jeanne, burdened by the strictures of her state of life and by her body's deformity:

> JEANNE:.... (*Silence.*) Mercy. (*Silence.*) I will find a way to You. I shall come. You will enfold me in Your sacred arms. The blood will flow between us, uniting us. My innocence is Yours.
>
> (p. 155)

Jeanne immediately reminds God of her hump, which prevents her lying at ease in bed. The combination of presences in her prayerful thoughts—deformity, piety, and desire for Christ—is expressed in a mystic's yoking of the spirit and the flesh. Religious longing is subsumed into physical desire (and vice versa); a Christ is needed for sleeping with: Grandier. Interestingly, human desire finds its best expression in the Cross of Christ (p. 154); possession thus becomes the obverse of crucifixion, making the intended object of sexual desire into a figure of the Christ.

Whiting brilliantly cuts back and forth between Jeanne and Grandier, who is busy coaching Phillipe in Latin translation; not surprisingly, the erotic texts produce their intended results, confessions of "Inclinations towards sin" (pp. 155-56). A blackout deprives us of watching their relationship enter its predictable next stage, but we are shown almost at once a Jeanne who has decided to ask Grandier to be her convent's confessor, for he has been much in her thoughts of late. Whiting thus manipulates his audience's double attention to both a truncated, but arguably subconciously ongoing, scene and another in which the climax of that first scene is reflected in an act of choice. We can follow Jeanne's projection of Grandier as the Christ of her dreaming; and in a remarkable stylistic adaptation of what now becomes projection in its cinematic sense, Whiting has Jeanne soliloquize upon a childhood memory of innocent and joyous physicality:

> JEANNE: A summer morning. Children playing. Boy and girl. Paper boats sail the pond. Sun shone so hot upon the head that day. Children crouched, staring at each other across the sheet of water. Was it love? Flick. A toad upon a slab. Croak. Boy, head to one side, smiling, gentle voice whispering over the water: Look. Speak to your brother, Jeanne. There. Green brother.

Hophop. Speak to him, Jeanne. (*Laughter: silence.*) God, forgive
my laughter. But you haven't given me much defence, have You?
(pp. 158-59)

Upon completing this filmic scene, Jeanne goes immediately to
her window, throwing it open to behold Grandier below at the
peak of his glory, "magnificent, golden, in the dying light of
day". The sight is too much: she cries out in agony, but
Grandier does not see the owner of the voice (p. 159). The die is
cast; the action of the play speeds downhill now, its course
predictable.

Jeanne writes out her invitation to Grandier. Adam and
Mannoury speak of the necessity of writing another paper,
Grandier's indictment. Phillipe confesses her lustful desires to
Grandier, mixing as she does his identity with that of her
unnamed imagined lover (pp. 159-61). The action of the play
moves swiftly now, one crucial commitment following upon
another. Not even De La Rochepozay's Shavian digression into
the dangers of a democratic frame of mind can swerve the play
from its collision-course (p. 162). In the very next scene Jeanne
is informed of Grandier's refusal, and in her anguish she
imagines Grandier and Phillipe naked together, making love. It
is an extraordinary scene: as if in epic theatre, Jeanne's
imagination works the strings of their amorous puppetry. It is a
masturbatory fantasy in which Jeanne "experiences" what she
wishes for herself, becoming (at least in voice) "young" in the
process, just as the lovers strike her as youthful during their
activities (pp. 162-63). In the space of a few dramatic moments,
however, Jeanne has managed to change this episode into
something more tolerable, less guilt-producing: she decides she
has been visited by Grandier, or by his spirit, and has heard him
speak "filth" to her (pp. 165-66).

Grandier is then seen in his pulpit, speaking out against his
enemies and accusers (p. 166), but he is truly ashamed only
when Phillipe speaks to him honestly and simply of her feeling
for him, one which he should not hesitate to show to God
directly. The first act ends, with a dramatic effect reminiscent of
Miller, as Jeanne makes an open accusation against Grandier
(pp. 169-70); but Whiting opens the second act with the
nocturnal wedding of Grandier and Phillipe (p. 171), an

178

affirmation that proceeds directly from Phillipe's earlier statement of faith (pp. 167-68). Thus a momentum is gathered up from Act I to open Act II, and Whiting sustains at least three temporarily disparate lines of dramatic involvement in moving his play along.

Act II is, however, largely a holding action, a section filled with philosophising and plot-thickening. Against the reliable doubtings of the Sewerman, Grandier propounds a new doctrine of hope: "There is a way of salvation through each other", he claims; one can come to God "by way of a fellow being", "reach God by way of happiness" (pp. 172-73). He can even put aside his pride enough to ask the "superior" Sewerman—superior because of the insight his level of existence and experience has given him—to pity him. The Sewerman's view of human nature animates the next scene, in which Jeanne is seen undergoing the rigours of exorcism at the hands of the manic Barré. Grandier, still not totally aware of the danger he is in, spares Jeanne and others like her some pity of his own: an understanding of their psychosexual situation that is quite intelligently accurate in its premises, however limited in its emotional commitment (p. 177). But Grandier does not yet know the extent of Jeanne's imaginings.

The next scene tells us: Jeanne describes for her inquisitors an assignation with Grandier in the convent chapel. During this invention (pp. 178-80), which Jeanne admits is based on reading, she presents a picture of voluptuous luxury accompanied by blasphemous defilement of holy things (she completes the scenario by remembering the presence of thorns, as if to run the pleasure-pain gamut in a particularly sacrilegious way). In an accompanying scene of related value-inversion, Phillipe reveals the fact of her pregnancy to Grandier, who finds that the revelation destroys the effect of their love. Now he is as one already dead; but before that, there had been a vision of a transcendental physicality:

> GRANDIER: I was filled with that indecent confidence which comes after perfect coupling. And as I went I thought—yes, solemnly I thought—the body can transcend its purpose. It can become a thing of such purity that it can be worshipped to the limits of imagination. Anything is allowed. All is right. And such

179

perfection makes for an understanding of the hideous state of existence.

(pp. 181-82)

This is the faith that Grandier has lost, and that he is to regain shortly before his death.

This loss of faith confirms Grandier's self-disdain. Now he wishes only to be "united with God", for living has drained him of the "need for life" (p. 184). Cut off by his enemies, he is in danger of his own death, as D'Armagnac warns him (p. 184)—a version of the fourth temptation offered Eliot's Becket. As he had once seen others as a means to God, he now looks upon them as a possible way of speeding his death along; the same end, perhaps, but now no longer looked upon with joyous anticipation. He cries out now to his God, like Christ upon the cross, feeling himself to be totally "forsaken" (p. 185). In the face of stereotyped human enemies (Barré: "My dear friend, a whisper from hell and I shall be back"; p. 183), the true struggle in *The Devils* is within the characters of its two principals, for it is there that God and the devils are born. Jeanne, for instance, speaks eloquently of the vanity of poor human pretensions: mankind, asking love of everything but God, and making itself ridiculous in the process, "For they do not understand the glory of mortality, the purpose of man: loneliness and death" (p. 186). It is thus left to Jeanne, who will end this play calling upon Grandier (like the Pegeen Mike who has lost the only playboy of the western world), to define a tragic conception of Man in a play that offers a comic alternative, natural love. But it does not do so any longer; Grandier receives the news that his political struggle has been lost by offering gratitude to God for giving his enemies strength and himself hope. Yet he asks God "Reveal Yourself. Reveal Yourself"; for God works behind a "curtain of majesty" that his eyes cannot penetrate (p. 187).

Much of the remainder of this second act is filled out with theatricality of the most engaging kind. We have the bizarre behaviour of the possessed nuns (pp. 189-95), eager to put on an appropriately convincing show for their inquisitors, among them the absurd Barré, who claims to speak for "the Lord Jesus Christ" although he is "only a humble man" (p. 190). We have the devils speaking in various and often witty voices. We have

the "exquisite and handsome sodomite", De Condé, with his
battery of "painted boys", his disdain of womankind, and his
clever demonstration of the faking of the possession exhibition
(p. 191). And we have, finally, the mass possession of
practically everyone on stage, priests included—but not, we
note, Jeanne (p. 194). This is the sensationalism on which the
appeal of the Loudon story is presumably based, and Whiting is
playwright enough to allow it free reign for a time.

It is De Condé, who has proved the devils fraudulent (for the
moment) with a purported phial of "the blood of our Lord Jesus
Christ", who warns the abstracted Jeanne that the punishment
for her course of action is having to give her "immortal soul to
damnation in an infinite desert of eternal bestiality". This is an
unusual warning to come from one such as De Condé, whom
Whiting makes an ironic *raisonneur* during Act II; but
De Condé, born high, has had to "stoop lower than other men"
and having "soiled, dabbling" himself, he knows what he is
talking about (p. 191). Thus a man who has been to the moral
equivalent of the Sewerman's realm is allowed to give Jeanne
vital caution, and she does indeed react with repeated claims
that she still wants to be "pure"—though she finally joins her
voice, as Leviathan, in an obscene giggling over the undignified
nature of human sexuality (pp. 195-96). And it is De Condé
who defends Grandier's right to have his private sexuality
preserved from public scrutiny in the presence of Richelieu,
asking for decent behaviour in the name of their "love of Jesus
Christ" (pp. 196-97). Whiting makes consistent use of the
device of value-inversion throughout *The Devils*.

This usage continues in the scene immediately following. In
it, Grandier tells of having ministered to a dying old man, and of
how the thought of that final reduction of humanity, along with
the memory of his "friend" the Sewerman, led him to a
remarkable epiphany. With the Sewerman listening quietly,
Grandier tells of how he "created" God:

> GRANDIER: I created Him from the light and the air, from the
> dust of the road, from the sweat of my hands, from gold, from
> filth, from the memory of women's faces, from great rivers, from
> children, from the works of man, from the past, the present, the
> future and the unknown. I caused Him to be from fear and
> despair. I gathered in everything from this mighty act, all I have

181

known, seen and experienced. My sin, my presumption, my
vanity, my love, my hate, my lust. And last I gave myself and so
made God. And he was magnificent. For He is all these things.

(p. 199)

And so Grandier gave himself Holy Communion there,
kneeling by the roadside. Finishing the story, concluding that
now he has found peace and meaning, he takes his leave of the
Sewerman, intending to enter his church. As he does, he is
arrested, and the sound of the devils is heard throughout the
town (pp. 199-200). Can Grandier's assuredness survive this
test?

Act III opens with just that question. Jeanne reveals that she
has Grandier within her; "Like a child" he is "lying beneath my
heart, living through my breath and my blood" (p. 202). And so
she calls out in the anguish of the knowledge that she may have
committed a grave evil. Grandier, too, is waiting in his cell.
Fearing that the pain to come will "kill God" in him, he reverts
to a far less attractive view of the human condition: "We are
flies upon the wall. Buzzing in the heat. That's so. That's so.
No, no. We're monsters made up in a day. Clay in a baby's
hands . . ." (p. 202). He questions his discovery of that morning,
and finds a "Nothing" within him, with no "meaning" left.
Then old Father Ambrose arrives, a patent faith-restoring
device whom Whiting shamelessly uses to bring back
Grandier's "meaning" in a trice. Almost disturbingly humble
and simple, Ambrose enters the play only to reaffirm Grandier
in his own earlier tenets of belief. If you have lived according to
the senses, he says, then die by them as well: "Offer God pain,
convulsion and disgust." We must go to God as we are; "All is
forgiven." This brief scene of Grandier's doubting is perhaps
intended to add some spark of light to a rapidly darkening play,
but there is something pat about Ambrose's appearance, and
also about Grandier's self-reassurance which follows: "For God
is here" (p. 205).

Nonetheless, the stripping and shaving of Grandier are now
ordered, a Christlike debasement that seems intended to
deprive him of pride and his sense of manhood (p. 207). Of
those who condemn him to death he begs some mitigation of his
sentence, for he fears falling into despair; denied this, he cites
his childhood admiration of Christ's martyrs and states his

182

intention of suffering, if not in hope of joining them, then at least in atonement for his life. Yet Grandier's mission, so conceived, is in effect an emulation of Christ in justification of a seemingly un-Christlike existence (p. 209). Perhaps to sustain the dramatic tension inherent in the moments of suspense before the death of Grandier, Whiting has De Laubardemont portray an horrific version of the suffering to come, warning Grandier in the process of the dangers of despair, and of the possibility of rejecting God out of pain (pp. 210-11). But it is Jeanne who is near despair, for she is next seen wandering about with a rope about her neck. If her distraction reminds us of Lady Macbeth, her role is closer to Judas's; she has betrayed her Christ, and recalls "the innocence of Christ" in reproving a nun who has disparaged Grandier (pp. 212-13). Jeanne has not yet reached her personal nadir, but Grandier is already rising from the depth of his.

So that when they torture him to make him confess his commerce with devils, he admits only to having been a man, a lover, a proud seeker after power. Jeanne, simultaneously, wonders how far she must fall, and whether God will be there when she touches bottom. "Is God here?" she asks, to the sound of Grandier's screams to God not to abandon him. God does not; if Grandier is to die for his own sins, his own devils, still he will die in possession of himself, and thus of his God. He is by this means made a type of Christ. Indeed, as he gazes down at the shattered remains of his body's lower regions, he quotes, in Latin, Lamentations 2:12, "behold, and see if there be any sorrow like unto my sorrow", lines from the Holy Office for the pre-Easter season which any priest would recognize as an identification of the sufferer with Christ. And as he does so, poor Jeanne wanders out, still crying, "Where are You? Where are You?" She has implicitly identified God and Christ with Grandier, yet she does not do so explicitly. In this extraordinary scene (pp. 213-15), performed to the sound of hammering, the certifying of Grandier as Whiting's Christ-figure is completed. As in *The Father*, a bystander—Barré—makes an error when the Christ-figure calls upon God; Barré mistakes the devil for Grandier's God. To complete the resemblance, Whiting has Grandier refuse to make a gesture of penitence for the sake of the Church, and instead warn of those "who will come after" him (pp. 215-16). In effect, Grandier is promising, in a way which is scarcely naturalistically justified, to complete his role of Christ by founding his own sort of Church.

The shattered body of Grandier is brought to Jeanne's convent so that he may beg forgiveness of the nuns he has supposedly wronged, and the arrival makes possible the only full physical meeting between Grandier and Jeanne. He wears a yellow shirt, and looks like a "ridiculous, hairless, shattered doll". It is a funereal scene accompanied by drum, bell, and a chorus singing the *Dies Irae*. The exchange of words between the two "lovers" is a telling one, and sums up the values of the play:

> JEANNE: They always spoke of your beauty. Now I see it with my own eyes and I know it to be true.
> GRANDIER: Look at this thing which I am, and learn the meaning of love.

(p. 217)

Again, naturalistic plot logic would point out that Jeanne has just admitted never having laid eyes on Grandier before, but the point is past mattering, and the admission, in any case, is "private". Indeed, it is the distance from naturalistic expression which gives the exchange its force and resonance. Grandier is beautiful in a way he never was when so proud of his appearance, and now his broken form has become an emblem of love, one which will have imprinted itself upon Jeanne's spirit like the visage of Christ upon Veronica's veil (p. 217). But the figure of a woman whose notion of love has been changed forever by a Christ belongs not so much to a Veronica as to a Mary.

The remaining pages of the play (pp. 218-20) show a Loudon which has become a Boschian nightmare scene; Jeanne wanders the streets while the population runs amuck. The grotesque Barré assures us that "men of our kind will never lack employment" (p. 219). Phillipe, who has married an old man, passes by; her version of the lesson of love is to promise ("Jesus, I will") to be a compliant and helpful lover to her aged spouse, who has become sexually excited by the execution festivities. Grandier's death has taught repentance and love by reason of its heroic scale. And D'Armagnac has been collecting strange sights; one of the odder things he has witnessed (one thinks of

Orpheus Descending) is a "musician crucified upon the harp".
Myth has coupled with myth in this play. Now we are reduced
to two characters again, the Sewerman and Jeanne. He tells her
how they made an ashen cross of Grandier's remains by
shovelling them to the four points of the compass, and he offers
Jeanne a charred bit of Grandier's bones. The townsfolk are
using them as charms, "for love or hate"; does Jeanne want it
for anything? No. Bones are no good for anything. She cries out
her beloved's name. The play ends.

Grandier, martyr-priest, seems to stand for values rather
different from those of Eliot's Thomas à Becket, but it is
essentially the same story, told from a different angle of vision.
The pattern persists in both. Though it might at first seem to
parody the values of the Christian Church that it mocks, *The
Devils* affirms an ancient notion: that we learn to love the God in
us by loving the us in each other. When we accomplish this
latter mission, we can confront what is arguably the even more
difficult task of learning to cope with the conflicts inherent in
our own natures. Because modern drama has tended to focus on
this interior dimension of the individual, its playwrights from as
far back as Ibsen through to Whiting and beyond have
persisted in discovering in the vestiges of their religious
consciousnesses the intuition that we need, in order to reconcile
the warring natures within us, the figure of a Christ.

NOTE

1 John Whiting, *The Devils*, in Ronald Hayman, ed., *The Collected Plays of
John Whiting*, Vol. 2 (New York, 1969). All page references appear
parenthetically within my text.

Index

187

188